THE INSTITUTE OF PACIFIC RELATIONS

The Institute of Pacific Relations is an unofficial and non-political organization, founded in 1925 to facilitate the scientific study of the peoples of the Pacific area. It is composed of autonomous National Councils in the principal countries having important interests in the Pacific area, together with an International Secretariat. It is privately financed by contributions from National Councils, corporations and foundations. The Institute, as such, does not advocate policies or doctrines and is precluded from expressing opinions on national or international affairs. It is governed by a Pacific Council composed of members appointed by each of the National Councils.

In addition to the independent activities of its National Councils, the Institute organizes private international conferences every two or three years. Such conferences have been held at Honolulu (1925 and 1927), Kyoto (1929), Shanghai (1931), Banff, Canada (1933), Yosemite Park, California (1936), Virginia Beach, Virginia (1939), Mont Tremblant, Quebec (1942). It conducts an extensive program of research on the political, economic and social problems of the Pacific area and the Far East. It also publishes the proceedings of its conferences under the title *Problems of the Pacific*, a quarterly journal *Pacific Affairs*, and a large number of scholarly books and pamphlets embodying the results of its studies.

NATIONAL COUNCILS

Australian Institute of International Affairs
Canadian Institute of International Affairs
China Institute of Pacific Relations
Netherlands—Netherlands Indies Council, Institute of Pacific Relations
New Zealand Institute of International Affairs
Philippine Institute of International Affairs
Royal Institute of International Affairs
U.S.S.R. Council, Institute of Pacific Relations
American Council, Institute of Pacific Relations

INTERNATIONAL SECRETARIAT AND PUBLICATIONS OFFICE
129 East 52nd Street, New York

THE JAPANESE IN SOUTH AMERICA

An Introductory Survey With Special Reference to Peru

BY

J. F. NORMANO

AND

ANTONELLO GERBI

I. P. R. INTERNATIONAL RESEARCH SERIES

*Issued in cooperation with the
Latin American Economic Institute*

INTERNATIONAL SECRETARIAT
INSTITUTE OF PACIFIC RELATIONS
129 East 52nd Street, New York
1943

Library of Congress Cataloging in Publication Data

Normano, João Frederico, 1890-1945.
　　The Japanese in South America.

　　　Reprint of the 1943 ed. published by the
International Secretariat, Institute of Pacific
Relations, New York and issued in cooperation
with the Latin American Economic Institute in
I.P.R. international research series.
　　A supplement to Trans-Pacific relations of
Latin America, by Anita Bradley.
　　Bibliography: p.
　　1. Japanese in South America.　2. Japanese
in Peru.　I. Gerbi, Antonello, 1904-
joint author.　II. Latin American Economic
Institute.　III. Bradley, Anita. Trans-
Pacific relations of Latin America.　IV. Title.
V. Series: Institute of Pacific Relations.
International research series.
F2239.J3N6　　1978　　　980'.004'956　　75-30075
ISBN 0-404-59550-2

First AMS edition published in 1978.

Reprinted from the edition of 1943, New York. [Trim size has been slightly altered in this edition. Original trim size: 12.2 x 19.2 cm. Text area of the original has been maintained.]

MANUFACTURED
IN THE UNITED STATES OF AMERICA

PREFACE

THE political and social significance of large colonies of Japanese in parts of South America has long been a subject of lively, if not always well-informed, controversy. To Brazil and Peru particularly it was a matter of some moment even before the present war broke out in the Pacific; now that all but one of the South American nations have severed relations with the Axis powers and Brazil is actually at war with Germany and Italy, though not as yet with Japan, the problem acquires an altogether new importance. Yet here, as in so many other aspects of this war, the United Nations have been singularly ill-provided with the basic information on which to make intelligent judgments or formulate wise policies. Many of the essential facts about the Japanese in South America are still unknown or else inaccessible to most readers. In the last twelve months or so several government agencies have done something to remedy this situation but unfortunately their studies do not, as a rule, reach the general public.

This modest study, as its sub-title "Introductory Survey" indicates, does not claim to provide answers to all, or even all the most important, questions at issue. That would have called for extensive field investigations and more time and funds than were available for this project. It is no more than a first attempt to awaken a wider and more intelligent public interest in the problem by sketching some of the salient general facts and giving a somewhat detailed first-hand picture of the relatively simple situation in Peru. It is fully recognized that the larger and more complicated situation in Brazil requires more thorough analysis than has been possible here, but it is hoped that with this introduction other research workers may be led to undertake such an inquiry and also that similar studies will be made of the Japanese in other Latin American countries. It will be apparent from this book that there will be considerable difficulties in making such studies, as statistics are far from adequate or reliable and much of the evidence is conflicting. The important task of examining the Japanese literature also awaits a careful research worker.

The book is intended as a supplement to the previous I.P.R. study, *Trans-Pacific Relations of Latin America,* by Anita Bradley. It is issued in cooperation with the Latin American Economic Institute, of which Dr. J. F. Normano is Research Director. To Dr. Normano must go the credit for initiating the study and for securing Dr. Gerbi's valuable essay. The first part of the book is based on Dr. Normano's more comprehensive manuscript on the Japanese in Latin America; thanks are due to Mr. Bruno Lasker of the Institute of Pacific Relations staff for his editorial work in condensing this longer report. Acknowledgments are also due to Mr. Walter B. Briggs of the Widener Library, Harvard University, to officials of several Latin American governments, to the Latin American Economic

PREFACE vii

Institute for its generous cooperation in the project, and to several Brazilian friends who have supplied information to Dr. Normano. Though the book appears under the joint auspices of the Institute of Pacific Relations and the Latin American Economic Institute, neither organization accepts responsibility for statements of fact or opinion herein; for all such statements the authors alone are responsible.

New York W. L. HOLLAND
February 1943 *Research Secretary*

CONTENTS

PART I—INTRODUCTORY SURVEY

I. JAPANESE MIGRATION TO LATIN AMERICA 3
    Immigration Legislation in Latin America 5
    Character of Japanese Immigration 9
    Trade and Migration 9
    From Trade War to War 18

II. THE JAPANESE IN BRAZIL 19
    Beginnings of Japanese Immigration 19
    Organization of Japanese Emigration 23
    Volume of Migration to Brazil 33
    THE JAPANESE COLONIES IN BRAZIL 35
    Organization of Settlements 37
    Principal Economic Activities 39
    Emigration as Part of Capitalistic Expansion 43
    Popular Attitudes Toward Japanese Immigration 47
    TRADE AND INVESTMENT 53
    WAR AND THE FUTURE 56
    POSTSCRIPT 57

PART II—THE JAPANESE IN PERU

I. THE PAST 61
    Early Contacts 61
    Developments Before 1914 66
    From 1914 to 1939 74

II. THE PRESENT 82
    Demographic Aspects 82
    Economic Aspects 85

III. TRADE WITH JAPAN 102
    General Characteristics 102
    Exports 104
    Imports 107
    Other Items in the Balance of Payments 110

IV. ANTI-JAPANESE LEGISLATION 113
    Immigration Restrictions 113
    Trade Restrictions 117

V. CONCLUSION 122
    BIBLIOGRAPHY 127

LIST OF TABLES

PART I

1A. Japanese Departures to Latin America, 1903-23 6
1B. Japanese Departures to Latin America, 1924-37 6
2. Japanese Residing Abroad, October 1, 1938 11
3. Japanese Residing in North and South America, 1925-38 11
4. Japanese Residing Abroad in Brazil and Peru and the World.. 12
5. Japanese Residents (Males and Females) in Brazil and Peru, 1925-38 12

CONTENTS

6.	Occupations of Japanese in South America, October 1, 1937 ...	12
7.	Japanese Trade with South America	15
8.	Japanese Trade with Principal Latin American Countries	16
9.	Nationality of Immigrants into Brazil, 1930 and 1939	34
10.	Japanese and Total Number of Immigrants into Brazil, 1933-1939	34

PART II

Arrivals and Departures of Japanese Citizens 74
Trade of Peru with Japan 102
Trade between Japan and Peru 103
Peruvian Bank Transactions in Yen and Hongkong Dollars 111

Part I

INTRODUCTORY SURVEY
By J. F. Normano

I. JAPANESE MIGRATION TO LATIN AMERICA

JAPANESE emigration to Latin America began to take on noteworthy dimensions only after admission to the United States was impeded by anti-Japanese agitation and especially after the passage of the so-called exclusion law of 1924. Emigration to Spanish South America began with the hiring of contract laborers and at first was directed almost entirely to Peru. After 1924, insignificant attempts were made also to send to Spanish America agriculturists who would form colonies carefully planned in advance.

This type of migration, however, developed into an important movement only when the attention of the Japanese authorities turned from Spanish to Portuguese South America, from Peru to Brazil. Because of the interesting contrasts between the two types of migration and between the receptions accorded them, the present study will consist, in the main, of comparative statements about Japanese experiences in the two countries named.

The general history of Japanese emigration has been discussed in a number of scholarly studies—all of which stress the connection of each change in policy or in direction with internal economic and political conditions in Japan, even though an active demand for Japanese labor played its part. Information on the nature and consequences of that emigration is fullest, of course, for those receiving countries in which the techniques of social studies are most fully developed. For Latin America, which has been among the most recent recipients of Japanese immigration, no comprehensive body of data has ever been published.[1]

Although its beginnings lie much farther back, planned and controlled Japanese migration to Latin America may be said to have its beginning with the exclusion of Japanese newcomers from the English-speaking countries, especially the United States. A trickle of irregular Japanese migration to the southern continent during the period of the Gentlemen's Agreement became a regular current after the Immigration Law of 1924. This law, in refusing admission to Orientals, was regarded in Japan as directed specifically against nationals of that country (Chinese immigration to the United States having been prohibited in 1882) and so became one of the causes of that mounting ill-feeling which seventeen years later found its vent at Pearl Harbor.

Whether Japanese statesmen considered themselves obliged to find new outlets for "surplus population" when those in North America were closed may be a matter for conjecture. More probably, considerations of trade and even of military strategy dictated a move

[1] For historical data and other supplementary information, including a selected bibliography, the reader is referred to Anita Bradley, *Trans-Pacific Relations of Latin America*, Institute of Pacific Relations, New York, 1941.

which, from the standpoint of population policy, would at best have offered only a very slight and rather costly form of relief.

The shift in the relative importance of North and South America as destinations of Japanese emigrants is dramatically told in the following round figures of Japanese residing in the Americas:

	1913	1928	1938
North America	319,000	170,000	142,000
South America	16,000	98,000	201,000

The change in the relative importance of Latin America among the destinations of total Japanese emigration is indicated by the figures in Table 1 (p. 6).

Immigration Legislation in Latin America

The general spirit of the immigration policy of the Latin American countries from the time of their independence up to World War I was one of enthusiastic encouragement. Economic motives stimulated this policy, as the smallness of the continent's population arrested the development of its resources. This policy was typified in the famous decree on immigration issued in Peru by Felipe Santiago Salavery in 1835. According to this decree, "every individual from any point of the globe is a citizen of Peru from the moment when, entering its (Peru's) territory, he wishes to be inscribed in the civil register." In the middle of the Nineteenth Century the great Argentine J. B. Alberdi expressed the essence of this immigration policy in Latin America in the words: "To govern is to popu-

THE JAPANESE IN SOUTH AMERICA

TABLE 1A. JAPANESE DEPARTURES TO LATIN AMERICA, 1903-23

Year	World Total	Latin America	Mexico	Brazil	Peru	Argentina
1903	14,055	1,710	281	—	1,303	126
1904	14,663	1,261	1,261	—	—	—
1905	13,302	346	346	—	—	—
1906	36,124	6,325	5,068	—	1,257	—
1907	25,060	3,908	3,822	—	85	1
1908	10,447	3,679	—	799	2,880	—
1909	4,278	1,145	2	4	1,138	1
1910	6,951	1,401	5	911	483	2
1911	8,071	494	28	—	456	2
1912	14,912	3,606	16	2,859	714	16
1913	20,966	8,250	47	6,947	1,126	103
1914	17,974	4,743	35	3,526	1,132	41
1915	12,543	1,447	19	39	1,348	33
1916	14,586	1,637	22	35	1,429	135
1917	22,862	6,036	53	3,883	1,948	127
1918	23,574	7,975	128	5,956	1,736	134
1919	18,244	4,501	64	2,732	1,507	174
1920	13,541	1,922	53	970	836	42
1921	12,944	1,835	69	970	717	53
1922	12,879	1,328	77	986	202	52
1923	8,825	1,271	68	796	333	66

TABLE 1B. JAPANESE DEPARTURES TO LATIN AMERICA, 1924-37

Year	Brazil	Peru	Argentina	Mexico	Total World Departures
1924	3,689	651	58	76	13,098
1925	4,908	922	121	160	10,696
1926	8,599	1,250	182	336	16,184
1927	9,625	1,271	262	319	18,041
1928	12,002	1,410	387	353	19,850
1929	15,597	1,585	430	249	25,704
1930	13,741	813	489	434	21,828
1931	5,565	299	362	283	10,384
1932	15,108	369	239	149	19,028
1933	23,299	480	135	85	27,317
1934	22,960	473	112	80	28,087
1935	5,745	814	201	53	10,813
1936	5,357	593	349	62	11,119
1937	4,675	166	307	65	10,744

Source: Japanese Foreign Office statistics and Ferenczi, *International Migrations*, p. 938. In some years there were large return movements: e.g. from Brazil 14,735 (1927), 5,402 (1928), 6,127 (1930), 2,367 (1931).— *Editor.*

late." Accordingly, these countries never knew restrictions of immigration prior to the World War.

The demand for labor, never satisfied, led to special efforts to attract Asiatic immigrants. All over Latin America, the possibilities of importing Asiatic labor were discussed. The abolition of the African slave trade had encouraged the importation of Chinese coolies, and the Asiatic laborer had already become a familiar figure in Latin American economy.

Some attention had been given also to Japanese immigration, in the latter part of the Nineteenth Century. In Mexico, Diáz Covarrubias as early as 1874 advocated the attraction of Japanese to Mexico. But only the beginning of the Twentieth Century witnessed a Japanese response to this desire. Japanese emigration to Spanish America was incidental and quantitatively negligible until the anti-Japanese agitation in the United States closed that country's doors to it. But even before the passage of the exclusion law, and before the Gentlemen's Agreement of 1907 curbed the influx of Japanese migrants to the United States, doubt as regards the wisdom of an unrestricted admission of Japanese had arisen here and there in Latin America. This distrust was sharpened by the growing signs of Japanese expansion policies, stimulated by the burst of national pride that had followed the victory over Russia. By 1910, Japanese missions and agents were to be found all over Spanish America, studying conditions and preparing the field for immigration.

The countries of Central America were the first to introduce restrictions against Asiatic immigration—

Costa Rica in 1896, Guatemala in 1909. Paraguay, Colombia, and other South American republics followed. In the 'thirties, almost all Spanish South American nations had on their statute books either general or racially discriminatory limitations of immigration. Among the causes may be named, first, the resentment already mentioned over Japanese political successes in the Far East, which greatly added to the empire's political power and potential danger. Whatever there may have been of racial prejudice had been reinforced by the anti-Japanese agitation—and later anti-Japanese legislation—in the United States. There was local discontent with the rapid growth of the Asiatic population (especially in Mexico) and fear of "unfair competition" as a result of the economic disturbances incident to the World War which culminated in the economic depression of the 'thirties. Partly as a result of these latter influences, there was a decided growth of economic nationalism throughout Latin America, and this led to the introduction of general as well as specifically anti-Asiatic restrictions on immigration.

The dangers of unrestricted Chinese immigration had, of course, been realized earlier than those of Japanese immigration and accordingly led to earlier restrictive legislation. Moreover, several of the Spanish-American governments desired to avoid anything in the nature of a formal racial discrimination, in this following the practice of the British Dominions rather than that of the United States. As a result, there was no series of immigration laws openly directed against the

Japanese. Nevertheless, Spanish America could no longer be regarded as a haven for Japanese immigrants.

Character of Japanese Immigration

The changed public attitude toward Japanese immigration through the greater part of Spanish America is explainable, above all, with the change in the economic and social functioning of Asiatic residents. Welcomed originally as a much-needed labor supply for the large-scale production of commercial crops, many of the immigrants and of their children had by the end of the first quarter of this century shifted over into less arduous occupations. The trend is so general that one can almost conclude from the vocational statistics how old or how recent Asiatic immigration has been in any given country of Latin America. All this indicates that an emigration which started with the recruitment of adventurous young men for agricultural work has become more varied in vocational composition, so that a larger proportion of older men have come, bringing their wives. It also suggests a growing stability, and perhaps a growing prosperity, of the Japanese residents who were able to an increasing extent to send home for wives selected for them by their relatives (called "picture brides" because of the custom of a previous exchange of photographs).

Trade and Migration

Having so long lived in a world which regarded freedom to choose one's domicile as an inalienable human right, we are liable to forget how recent that freedom of movement is, even in Europe. In a large part of the world it has never been recognized, and since the beginning of the first World War it has in practice disappeared from many Western countries as they parted with other rights, too, that had been implied in the general principle of *laissez-faire*.

Japan has never known an epoch of real individualism. It jumped straight from the mercantilistic feudalism of Tokugawa into the more enlightened neo-mercantilism of the Meiji era. Both the volume and the direction of Japanese emigration, therefore, have always been under control, although there have been great differences in the degree to which the State organized and conducted migration movements as well as gave them direction. The evolution of policy in this respect has always been influenced primarily by economic considerations.

Study abroad was the first and most obvious departure from the traditional official discouragement of any foreign travel. Trade and labor opportunities abroad were recognized almost simultaneously as useful to the State, in the 'eighties. Protection of emigrants from abuse abroad produced the earlier emigration legislation; but in the course of decades, the Government felt itself more and more compelled to intervene in the organization of emigration itself, until finally, in the 'twenties, managed emigration was accepted as an important instrument of economic policy. It came to be more and more related to plans for the development of trade and, especially, of sources of raw materials to assist in the growth of industry at home.

JAPANESE MIGRATION TO LATIN AMERICA

TABLE 2. JAPANESE RESIDING ABROAD, OCTOBER 1, 1938

Country	Male	Female	Total	Total 1933
World (total)	598,490	461,423	1,059,913	749,158
Asia (total)	317,938	240,807	558,745	277,140
Manchuria	233,842	184,473	418,315	182,601
China Proper	54,379	41,129	95,508	55,064
Philippines	17,248	8,589	25,837	20,400
North America (total)	82,406	59,989	142,395	130,577
United States	67,039	48,734	115,773	103,765
Canada	13,140	9,905	23,045	20,393
Mexico	1,487	1,058	2,545	5,297
Hawaii	78,830	37,020	115,850	149,207
South America (total)	114,790	86,030	200,820	185,546
Brazil	95,116	75,049	170,165	157,476
Argentina	4,828	1,831	6,659	5,334
Uruguay	56	33	89	37
Paraguay	293	227	520	5
Peru	13,261	8,242	21,503	21,281
Bolivia	591	284	875	627
Chile	450	245	695	635
Colombia	175	114	289	144
Venezuela	20*	5*	25*	7

*October 1, 1937

Source: Japanese Foreign Office statistics in *Japan Year Book*.

TABLE 3. JAPANESE RESIDING IN NORTH AND SOUTH AMERICA, 1925-38

Year	North America	South America	World
1925	295,641	64,191	617,929
1928	169,569	98,037	709,838
1931	127,964	142,648	509,754
1932	131,152	146,678	635,227
1933	129,429	160,387	672,266
1934	174,230	201,740	872,807
1935	123,611	200,786	689,818
1936	137,587	223,655	997,115
1937	141,481	228,478	1,043,412
1938*	142,395	200,820[a]	1,059,913

*Estimate.

[a] This large reduction is unexplained and seems improbable.—*Editor*.

Source: Japanese Foreign Office statistics in *Japan Year Book*.

TABLE 4. JAPANESE RESIDING ABROAD IN BRAZIL AND PERU AND THE WORLD
(Numbers and Percent of World Total)

Year	Brazil	Percent	Peru	Percent	World
1904	5	—	1,486	1.1	138,591
1914	15,462	4.3	5,381	1.5	358,711
1920	33,456	6.2	5,910	1.1	541,784
1926	55,481	8.8	11,787	1.8	640,099
1929	103,166	13.0	18,041	2.3	795,018
1931	119,740	15.3	20,650	2.6	777,908
1933	157,476	21.0	21,281	2.8	749,158
1934	173,500	19.9	21,127	2.4	872,807
1936	193,057	19.8	22,570	2.3	977,115
1937	197,733	19.0	22,150	2.1	1,042,974
1938	170,165[a]	16.1	21,503	2.0	1,059,913

[a]This large unexplained decrease seems improbable. It may indicate some change in methods of enumeration.—*Editor.*
Source: Japanese Foreign Office statistics.

TABLE 5. JAPANESE RESIDENTS (MALES AND FEMALES) IN BRAZIL AND PERU, 1925-38

	Brazil		Peru	
Year	Male	Female	Male	Female
1925	27,336	22,064	7,897	3,095
1928	42,707	33,781	11,435	5,544
1931	68,112	51,628	13,301	7,349
1933	91,373	66,103	13,664	7,617
1936	107,682	85,375	14,280	8,290
1938	95,116	75,049	13,261	8,242

Source: Japanese Foreign Office statistics.

TABLE 6. OCCUPATIONS OF JAPANESE IN SOUTH AMERICA, OCTOBER 1, 1937

	Brazil	Peru	Argentina
Total Japanese	197,728	22,150	6,267
Percent in:	%	%	%
Agriculture	19.4	9.3	18.2
Manufacturing	0.5	2.1	20.3
Commerce	9.9	18.6	14.7
Domestic Work	0.2	0.5	2.2
Civil Service, etc.	3.4	0.7	0.9
Without occupation*	79.0	68.0	40.1

*Mostly members of families.
Source: *Japan Year Book.*

Tables 2 and 3 above, relating to the distribution of Japanese residents abroad, acquire additional significance if we compare them with the figures given below for both the actual growth of Japanese trade with Latin America and its proportion in the total foreign trade of Japan. The remakable fact about this trade has been not its size but the rapidity of its growth despite the economic depression which kept Japan's total foreign trade from rising correspondingly.

There has been a concentration of Japanese purchases in Latin America upon those countries, in the main, which also permitted a corresponding rise of Japanese imports—though the need for strategic raw materials obviously must have been the chief consideration.

The expansion of Japanese trade in Latin America in the early 'thirties has been widely regarded as not only an effort to make up for past neglect of that source and market but also as a deliberate trade war against Great Britain, in retaliation for the ban of certain Japanese commodities from British markets. This desire also would explain the readiness with which, despite a serious financial situation at home, Japan was able to find the means to invest in the establishment of colonies in South America, involving a considerable capital expenditure in behalf of each emigrant, not to mention added ship subsidies, the establishment of new trade offices abroad, and other investments not immediately remunerative.

World opinion, influenced by many reports, official and unofficial, by complaints from Chambers of Commerce, and by diplomatic communications, became aroused, especially in 1934 and 1935, over the Japanese trade mobilization in Latin America. Some newspapers spoke of a "trade war." The peak of the Japanese trade success in that region, however, was reached in 1937. A decline in 1938 and 1939 seems to have been fully made up in 1940. The proportion of Japan's part in the value of exports from twenty Latin American countries had risen from 0.1 per cent in 1929 to 2.0 per cent in 1936, the last year before Japan's efforts became absorbed in the war with China; its part in the value of imports to the same countries from 0.6 to 3.0 per cent.

The bulk of Japanese exports to Latin America consists of manufactured goods and products of light industries. Cotton textiles dominate, with silk and rayon following. Cotton textiles is the most competitive field in world trade and especially in Latin America because here Japan meets not only the rivalry of Great Britain and the United States but has to beat also the steadily growing native competition which in many cases has the advantage of being locally supplied with raw material. While the cotton crop in Brazil and especially in São Paulo owes much to the Japanese planters, the increasing industrialization leads to growth of the local manufacture of cotton goods. The same is the case, on a smaller scale, in Peru and Argentina.

The other important items of Japanese export to this part of the world are products of light industries like porcelains, toys, buttons, cosmetics, electric bulbs and appliances, and so on.

TABLE 7. JAPANESE TRADE WITH SOUTH AMERICA

Year	Total Trade of Japan (million yen) Exports	Imports	South America[a] (thousand yen) Exports to	Imports from
1900	198	287	3	11
1901	252	256	5	1
1902	258	272	2	—
1903	290	317	12	18
1904	319	371	5	2
1905	322	489	10	4
1906	424	419	50	52
1907	432	494	218	842
1908	378	436	126	631
1909	413	394	128	1,621
1910	458	464	272	1,926
1911	447	514	353	2,681
1912	527	619	1,766	1,862
1913	632	729	1,673	2,781
1914	591	596	510	2,626
1915	708	532	1,545	3,127
1916	1,127	756	2,994	6,746
1917	1,603	1,037	7,588	14,486
1918	1,962	1,668	36,893	20,878
1919	2,099	2,173	20,831	18,183
1920	1,948	2,336	39,098	32,112
1921	1,253	1,614	4,496	5,102
1922	1,637	1,890	10,360	7,575
1923	1,448	1,982	11,569	10,027
1924	1,807	2,453	18,056	8,535
1925	2,306	2,573	17,705	8,512
1926	2,045	2,377	16,831	11,944
1927	1,992	2,179	20,886	10,478
1928	1,972	2,196	21,130	12,199
1929	2,149	2,216	23,026	14,263
1930	1,470	1,546	16,415	6,835
1931	1,147	1,236	10,225	7,097
1932	1,410	1,431	12,133	4,680
1933	1,861	1,917	30,739	12,872
1934	2,172	2,283	61,457	23,962
1935	2,499	2,472	73,362	42,908
1936	2,693	2,764	68,761	112,190
1937	3,175	3,783	109,519	162,611
1938	2,690	2,663	60,151	91,235
1939	3,576	2,918	67,111	115,730

[a] Figures are for Chile and Peru only for 1900-1910.
Source: *Résumé Statistique de l'Empire du Japon*, and *Returns of the Foreign Trade of Japan*, Tokyo.

TABLE 8. JAPANESE TRADE WITH PRINCIPAL LATIN AMERICAN COUNTRIES (thousand yen)

	Brazil		Argentina		Uruguay	
	Exports	Imports	Exports	Imports	Exports	Imports
1931	642	452	4,700	2,901	1,150	686
1932	1,330	753	7,553	2,719	422	173
1933	2,765	1,008	12,261	6,738	2,451	317
1934	3,064	3,292	20,013	12,128	6,965	2,631
1935	5,926	4,006	28,602	16,371	5,678	4,495
1936	8,840	47,352	22,712	29,989	7,891	9,528
1937	17,305	62,810	42,481	42,018	10,106	33,926
1938	10,388	46,174	19,607	24,356	3,988	4,158
1939	15,609	74,662	8,152	11,860	3,771	3,398

	Peru		Chile		Venezuela	
	Exports	Imports	Exports	Imports	Exports	Imports
1931	800	17	804	2,942	—	—
1932	840	41	286	761	—	—
1933	3,899	1,553	1,475	2,962	—	—
1934	6,879	1,823	7,440	3,438	1,970	36
1935	6,961	11,415	6,647	4,473	3,565	56
1936	6,156	13,000	7,426	9,953	7,814	257
1937	6,344	6,277	10,742	14,719	9,139	231
1938	5,760	1,975	6,129	11,152	5,480	1,498
1939	6,084	6,956	14,010	10,230	7,984	129

	Mexico		Panama	
	Exports	Imports	Exports	Imports
1931	666	90	449	8
1932	638	318	551	35
1933	1,491	188	1,100	9
1934	4,010	857	4,250	20
1935	5,465	8,033	6,150	89
1936	7,190	21,791	9,546	17
1937	13,622	14,262	10,248	66
1938	5,317	4,703	6,227	9
1939	7,940	1,536	8,103	15

Source: *Returns of the Foreign Trade of Japan*, Tokyo.

In all her exports to Latin America, Japan had to fight legislative restrictions—administrative and tariff protection, boycott movements, and difficulties resulting from exchange control.[2]

The Japanese imports from Latin America consist almost exclusively of raw materials: raw cotton and wool on the top of the list, nitrates and copper, tin, petroleum, wheat, beef, hides and skins; in smaller quantities: sugar, tobacco, and coffee. Japan gave special attention to the import of raw cotton from Latin America in order to be independent of the United States' crop, and imported it from Brazil, Argentina, Peru. Its substantial wool imports from Argentina and Uruguay declined with the agreement with Australia and the rise of imports from Manchuria and China.

The entire decade of the 'thirties can be characterized as one of almost feverish attempts on the part of Japan to increase trade relations with Latin America. Even at the beginning of the second world war Japan officially declared her intentions to capture markets formerly controlled by Germany—at least that was supposed to have been the topic of the meeting in Washington of the entire diplomatic representation of Japan in North and South America in the spring of 1940.[3] But it is now clear that the true objective of Japan at that time was to import for accumulation and storage all kinds of raw materials having a distinct relationship to heavy industrial or military necessities.

[2] For a detailed report on these restrictions see U. S. Tariff Commission, *The Foreign Trade of Latin America*, Part I, Washington, D. C., 1940, pp. 21-27.

[3] *New York Herald Tribune*, June 9, 1940.

18 THE JAPANESE IN SOUTH AMERICA

From Trade War to War

While no figures are available for 1940-1941, even a superficial study of the daily press discloses that since the beginning of the second world war Japan launched not a trade war in Latin America but a fight for improvement of her war preparedness. The Japanese endeavored to obtain hides and wool from Rio Grande do Sul and sought to secure in Brazil large quantities of mica, crystal quartz, rubber, industrial diamonds, scrap iron, and other war materials. They tried to corner the markets; they used German funds and acted as German purchasing agents; they increased purchases of sugar and cotton in Peru; they took the whole of Peru's output of molybdenum, copper, and silver ores, antimony ore, tungsten ore, vanadium ashes—all strategic metals. Japanese vessels carried from Chile important lots of copper, low-grade minerals, and wools, and sought to obtain mercury, manganese, cobalt and other ores.[4]

Harold Callender, in his factual and instructive correspondence from all over Latin America in the first half of 1941, noticed and emphasized this tendency and expressed the suspicion that Japan was in these purchases acting as German agent and trying in this way to break the blockade. In most of the cases Japan willingly offered higher prices than the United States and was ready to accept ores of lower grade. It was the same situation everywhere in Latin America—in Chile, Peru, Bolivia, in any market where strategic materials were obtainable. Callender cited the increased buying

[4] *New York Times,* March 2, February 2, May 15, 1941, July 13, July 9, 1941.

in Peru: seven to ten Japanese ships a month put into the harbor, as compared with an average of two before the war.[5]

The *Christian Science Monitor* declared the Mexican metal market virtually cornered by Japan in 1940. The success of the Japanese activities has been explained by their overbidding other purchasers on all war supplies. A temporary Mexican embargo on shipments of metals to Japan lasted only three days. Mexico's oil was, of course, also available to Japan in unknown quantities. Heavy Japanese purchases of henequen, mercury, fluorspar, and other materials, likewise were reported from Mexico. When the war is over a future investigator will be able to add to its history an interesting chapter on the Japanese strategy of war materials.

II. THE JAPANESE IN BRAZIL

Beginnings of Japanese Immigration

The attitude of Portuguese America toward Asiatic and particularly Japanese immigration was analogous to that of Spanish America prior to the first World War. During her history Brazil had welcomed the immigration of many racial groups. Shortage of labor and underpopulation have been and are the weakest points of Brazilian economy. During the life of the Brazilian Empire the problem of Asiatic colonization was frequently discussed. Colonization by Chinese was attempted in the early years of the reign of Pedro II and

[5] *Ibid.* May 15, 1941.

again after the anti-slavery law of 1871. Salvador de Mendonça, then Brazilian Consul General in the United States, was ordered by his Government to investigate the possibilities of Asiatic emigration to Brazil.

After the emancipation of its slaves, Brazil sent a special mission to China to arrange with the Government for the organized importation of Chinese laborers, in order to mitigate the shock caused to the Brazilian labor market.

As early as 1896, the Brazilian Government negotiated also with Japan concerning immigration, but we do not possess any information concerning this attempt.[6]

Need for plantation labor has always been an economic stimulus in the history of colored migrations. In modern times, gold, sugar, coffee, cotton, and other products have had more to do with moving colored people from continent to continent than has any other cause. The crisis in the labor market in coffee production caused the Brazilian Government especially to welcome the first steps of Japanese immigration in the Twentieth Century. The insistence of the coffee *fazendeiros* led to the organized importation of Japanese contract laborers.

In the first quarter of the present century Italy represented one of the main sources of Brazilian immigration. From the time of the unification of that country until 1927 its Government encouraged emigration.

[6] R. A. Hehl, "Die Entwicklung der Einwanderungsgesetzgebung in Brasilien," in *Schriften des Vereins für Sozialpolitik,* Bd. LXXII, Leipzig, 1896, p. 293.

Since 1927, however, emigration has been considered an "evil," as Facism declares that man-power is one of the essential factors of political and moral power. Mussolini's change of the Italian emigration policy deprived Brazil of Italian immigrants. Thus, after the first World War Brazil did not adopt the restrictive immigration policy of several Spanish-American republics but continued to encourage Japanese immigration.

Instructions issued on June 30, 1925 gave to the Director of the Serviço Geral do Povoamento do Solo the right to suspend immigration or to limit it temporarily, but no use was made of this power. Since January 1931, the only immigrants allowed to land have been those whose entry has been solicited by the Federal Interventor, through the intermediary of the Minister of Labor, and those who hold a note of call (*bilhete de chamada*); also agriculturists who have satisfied certain requirements. Temporary migrants must be in possession of an amount equivalent to three contos of reis (about U. S. $160).

Obviously these restrictions did not affect the Japanese arriving under special contract and concession agreements. Indeed, the Brazilian Government consented to increase the number of Japanese immigrants.

Immigration legislation of July 1934 voted by the Constituent Assembly under the influence of propaganda started by Dr. Miguel Conto, restricted the entry of immigrants annually to 2 per cent of the total entries of the past fifty years. This famous Article 121 affected Japan more than any other country, in spite of the absence of any kind of formal discrimination. But the

Brazilian Government felt free to admit immediately after its introduction large numbers of Japanese colonists in exemption from this rule. Public opinion in Brazil became divided on restriction for Japanese. The nationalistic Alberto Torres Patriotic Society regarded the clause as a victory in its campaign to bar all Japanese immigration and considered it consistent with Alberto Torres' ideas preaching the Brazilianization of Brazil. At the same time, several Brazilian officials made statements deprecating what they called the "short-sighted view" of the anti-Japanists.

This seemingly favorable attitude was probably an attempt to pacify the infuriated Japanese Foreign Office. Foreign Minister Koki Hirota declared in the House of Representatives that the Brazilian restrictions would "leave a blot on the history of cordial relations" between the two countries. The Brazilian correspondent of *Nichi Nichi* complained that "the pressure of a certain power aggravated the situation." In addition, local Brazilian politics and especially the conflict between the most industrialized coffee state São Paulo and the Federal Government of Getulio Vargas found their repercussions in the attitude toward Japanese immigration.

In spite of all mildness in its administration at the beginning, the restriction of Japanese immigration to Brazil soon became serious. The years 1938 and 1939 brought further laws restricting the freedom of immigrants, declaring as one of the aims that aliens were to be prevented from being too much attached to their own language and their national customs. New settlements within 150 kilometres from the frontier of Brazil were prohibited. While directed against the entire Axis, the new regulations seriously affected the Japanese.

While objections to foreign colonies and incidental anti-Japanese outbursts could from time to time be found in previous nationalistic writings of some important Brazilian thinkers, like Silvio Romero and Alberto Torres, the resentment grew larger in the second decade of the 'thirties. Brazilian national consciousness and the will to "Brazilianize" the country caused public opinion as well as governmental policy to concentrate attention on unassimilable foreign elements. Brazilian sociologists support this trend, and the administration of the Estado Novo seems to exercise special watch through the numerous military and civil agencies of local, federal, and state authorities.

The Council on Immigration and Colonization created by President Vargas on May 4, 1938 devoted special attention to the German and Japanese colonies and undertook field studies of the settlements in connection with the aim of the new colonization policy to prevent "the formation of alien racial groups within the country which could be assimilated only with difficulty." No settlement may contain more than 25 per cent of aliens of any one nationality, and at least 30 per cent of every settlement must be Brazilian.

Organization of Japanese Emigration

After the opening of Japan to intercourse with the West, there was a short period of free emigration. But as soon as employers in foreign countries—notably Hawaii and continental United States—showed an interest in the employment of Japanese labor, Japan entered the field of both legal and economic regulation of emigration. This traditional paternalistic attitude was at first applied to contract workers, was extended to other classes when emigration to Spanish America grew in volume, and reached its climax in the deliberate planning, preparation, and organization of emigration to Portuguese America.

Most of the measures of control which are characteristic of the period after 1924 had originated in the previous period of large-scale emigration to the Pacific Coast of Spanish America—but there in milder, embryonic, and more experimental forms. After 1924, emigration became a matter almost entirely of governmental organization. As the experimental period marked the shifting of the movement from English-speaking to Spanish-speaking America, so the new one marked a shift to Portuguese America. We may call this the Atlantic period.

The governmental organization of Japanese emigration to Brazil was the first mass-experiment in the history of Japanese emigration. Before 1924, no special efforts were devoted to Brazil; all the measures taken applied to Spanish America as well. On the other hand, the new system was applied only to emigration to Brazil, and the latter is the only one which has attained large proportions.

As early as 1898, one of the Japanese emigration companies attempted to send contract emigrants to

Brazil; but large-scale emigration to Brazil dates only from 1907, when an agreement was signed between the Government of the State of São Paulo and a private Japanese corporation handling emigrants—the Kokoku Shokumin Kaisha, represented by Ryu Minumo, who previously visited Brazil and who has been called the "father of Japanese emigrants in Brazil." The company received a subsidy and was to send, during the three following years, three thousand Japanese between twelve and forty years of age, to be accompanied by their families. The emigrants were to be settled on the coffee plantations with houses provided by the landlords, and eventually they were to form colonies along the Brazilian Central Railroad. In the case of establishment of colonies, however, they were to buy on installment pieces of land of ten to fifteen hectares at a fixed price and the State then undertook to build houses for the colonists and supply them with the necessary equipment. This experiment did not succeed. The hundred and fifty-eight families of Japanese immigrants were absolutely ignorant of local conditions and ran into difficulties. The result was the bankruptcy of the Kokoku Colonization Company.

This experiment was followed on a small scale by the Takemura Shokumin Shokan, the Toyo Imin Goshi Kaisha, and the Nambei Shokumin Kabushiki, up to 1914, when the outbreak of the World War stopped migration from Europe to Brazil. The shortage of labor in that country led to a coordination of efforts on the part of the Japanese emigration companies. The Toyo Imin Goshi Kaisha, the Nambei Shokumin Kabushiki and Morioka Imin Kaisha organized jointly the Brazil Imin Kumiai, which entered into negotiations with the state of São Paulo for the transportation of five thousand contract laborers over a period of four years.

In 1917, the Minister of Finance, Kazue Shoda, sponsored the fusion of these five emigration companies into the Kaigai Kogyo Kabushiki Kaisha (the Overseas Development Company, Ltd.), with a capital of nine million yen. This company took over another corporation in 1920 and, by absorbing several other small companies, became virtually the sole emigration agency in Japan. This enterprise had its agents at various destinations of Japanese emigration, such as Australia and the South Sea Islands, also in Peru, Colombia, Cuba; but the bulk of the traffic was directed toward Brazil. By the end of 1930, the company had handled over 96,000 emigrants—about 73,000 of them to Brazil, 14,000 to the Philippines, and three thousand to Peru.

Under the direction of the Kaigai Kogyo Kaisha, emigration took on larger dimensions. Emphasis was transferred from contract-emigrants to colonist-settlers.

Before 1924 Japanese emigration to Brazil was not a large enterprise. Brazil was mentioned in the official reports only incidentally as one of the Latin American countries presenting a possible field for Japanese emigration. When in 1906 and 1907 the Japanese turned their eyes to Latin America, they had in mind the Pacific coast. The initiator of this movement, Count Okuma, in an interview with Professor E. A. Ross, as well as in an article published in 1907 in the Tokyo *Economist*, did not even mention Brazil. Mr.

Ichida, Japanese Minister to Brazil, only incidentally called attention to possibilities in Brazilian agriculture. The change came after the first World War. The Japanese War Investigating Committee included South America in its observations and sent numerous investigators there. Dr. Schuchart presents many instances of the feverish activity of various Japanese missions to Latin America during the war.[7] The Latin American newspapers of 1916-1919 are full of notes on Japanese visitors to Latin America. In the spring of 1919 three trade missions visited Mexico.

Simultaneously a number of trade-promoting organizations were established in Japan. The Japan-Chile Trade Association was formed at Tokyo in 1916, followed by a Latin American-Japanese Society and a Japan-Mexico Society. Japan took an important part in the Panama-Pacific International Exhibition in Panama, organized a special industrial exhibition in Santiago de Chile, and established Japanese commercial museums in Buenos Aires and Santiago de Chile. But soon Japanese activity changed its direction.

In 1924 the Emigration Council, headed by Minister of Foreign Affairs Shidehara, sent a new mission to South America. As a result of this study, Japan concentrated her emigration efforts on Brazil. As soon as this decision was taken, the Japanese Government established a centralized, rationalized management of emigration to Brazil, initiating an organized intercontinental transplantation of human beings on a large scale.

[7] Schuchart, *Japans Rüstung für den Handelskrieg*, Berlin, 1918, p. 37.

A governmental subvention had been given to the Kaigai Kogyo Kaisha since 1921. The direct financial assistance to the company consisted of a yearly subsidy of a hundred thousand to two hundred fifty thousand yen plus a contribution amounting to the cost of passage of the emigrants. In 1927, when the Minister of the Interior was President of the Kaigai Kogyo Kaisha, a special Colonization Bank was established. From 1923, the Government provided in the budget for "emigration publicity," and Japanese legations and consulates were instructed to furnish information which would permit the Government to form an accurate estimate of the openings which different countries offer Japanese settlers. The Japanese Government, largely in cooperation with the Kaigai Kogyo Kaisha, organized a propaganda for emigration to Brazil. Taking into account the traditional Japanese attitude toward emigration, the propaganda did not report stories of an El Dorado but emphasized the resemblance between the prospective home in Brazil and the native village, assured the prospective migrant of possibilities to transplant the Japanese environment, and described the economic conditions as promising. Forty representatives of the Kaigai Kogyo Kaisha travelled all over the country lecturing and showing films of Japanese colonies in Brazil and conditions there.[8] The number of lectures on this subject rose from 27 in 1923 to 267 in 1930. For some years before the second world war most of the boys and girls in the schools of southern Japan saw on the screen, inter-

[8] Etienne Dennery, *Asia's Teeming Millions*, London, 1931, pp. 66-67.

spersed with comments from a Government lecturer, alluring pictures of country life in Brazil. Sometimes the pictures were shown in a continuous story with a very simple plot; the audience witnessed the departure of a peasant and his wife from the land of their ancestors and from their too restricted ricefield. But on the coffee plantation of Brazil, as shown on the screen, in a little wooden hut exactly like those of Japan, over which floats the flag of their country, life continued exactly the same as at home. According to the film, their fortune once made, the family came home again to the ricefield in the village, the tomb of their ancestors, and the little house bright with wisteria and the cherry tree in bloom. Special museums and exhibitions provided further information about the new home.

In 1915, Kaigai Kyokai (Overseas Societies) were formed in the prefectures of Hiroshima and Kumamoto. They were followed in 1918 by similar societies in other prefectures.

The Overseas Emigration Societies Act of 1927 provided for the establishment of emigration cooperative societies (Kaigai Iju Kumiai) on the lines of the old Japanese guilds. The purpose of these guilds was to form groups for joint emigration—groups with spiritual as well as economic ties. The guilds assisted the emigration of persons who possessed some capital which they could invest in land in the receiving country; in fact, one of their main purposes was the purchase of land in overseas countries. After this act came into effect, overseas emigration societies were formed in eighteen prefectures. The total number of members in these societies reached nearly ten thousand in 1931; in one prosperous society alone the membership exceeded 1,900. A further step toward centralization took place when a federation of these societies was formed in 1927. The Kagai Iju Kumiai Kengokai (The Association of Overseas Emigration Partnerships) had 51 members of which 37 were Kaigai Iju Kumiai. This association organized the Brazil Takahoka Kumiai which engaged in the acquisition of land for colonists in Brazil.

The candidates for emigration were selected from the members of the guilds. After an applicant had been selected, had received authorization, and had provided surety at home, he had to undergo a medical examination and training in a special emigrant school. The Portuguese language, tropical hygiene, tropical agriculture, civic behavior, and the elements of Brazilian geography, history and economy were the main features of the educational program. The emigrant had to represent Japan abroad—that is why his preparation for this service began at home. After this preliminary training, he was transferred to Kobe or Yokohama where he waited in the specially established Emigrants' Home for the steamer. Similar homes were established in the Brazilian ports of Santos and Belém.

The two chief Japanese steamship companies, the Nippon Yusen Kaisha (N.Y.K.) and the Osaka Shosen Kaisha (O.S.K.), divided the Latin American field in such a way that the N.Y.K. touched the Pacific and the O.S.K. the Atlantic ports. Both of them belong to the group of "Shasen"—steamship companies under special patronage of the Government in distinction from the unsubsidized or less subsidized "Shagai-sen." The "Shasen" companies comprise about 30 per cent of the Japanese gross tonnage and cover the regular routes prescribed by the Government. The pioneer of the South American route, the Toyo Kisen Kaisha (the first line to Peru in 1906 and to Mexico in 1910), which some years ago extended its line from Callao via Valparaiso and Buenos Aires to Brazil, was later taken over by the N.Y.K.

The subsidized Yokohama-Buenos Aires line of the O.S.K. brought the emigrants, still under supervision of the Kaigai Kogyo Kaisha, to their new home. On the arrival of the ship at the Brazilian port the staff of the local branch of the Kaigai Kogyo Kaisha received the immigrants into the home and after registration sent them to their place of destination.

The system of supervision and protection continues in Brazil. The laborer immigrant signs a contract for four years and does not receive any promise of payment for the return passage. He finds himself on the *fazenda* where he works among countrymen. After he accumulates some savings the company buys land for him, and he joins the colonists: The colonist immigrant on the other hand goes directly to a settlement with his group or joins some existing Japanese settlement.

Attention has been given to the smallest detail in order to avoid any clash with the native population. For instance, emigration of the Buddhist and Shintoist clergy is restricted, while that of the Roman Catholic is encouraged. The President of the Amazon Company, Hachiro Fukuhara, is a Catholic. Naturalization in Brazil is advocated. But registration with the Japanese Consulate and membership in one of the Japanese associations under the supervision of the consulate are required. In some schools, as for instance in the Colegio Niponico in Lins (São Paulo), only children of Japanese registered at the consulate are admitted. Brazilian observers state that the Japanese register births of children only with the representative of the consulate and not in the civil register. The representative is usually the local teacher and at the same time the clerk of the colony.

As in the United States, the Japanese immigrants in Brazil are more highly organized than any other national or racial group. Dennery explains this with the fact that the Japanese remain together in emigration by their feeling of superiority and tradition, in contrast with the Chinese who remain close to each other by their love of family and through business interests, and the Indians on the plantations by an inherited submissiveness.[9] Officers, physicians, and members of the consular service work on the *fazendas* in order to gain personal knowledge of conditions.

The newcomer has to do the work assigned to him. The Emigration Company provides everything else but insists on blind obedience. The colonists are headed by group leaders who are spokesmen between the laborers and the *fazendeiros* or captains of the colonies.[10] Japa-

[9] *Op. cit.*, p. 148.
[10] This group organization has its source in the old but still living Japanese institution of *Goningumi*—an association of nominally five, but sometimes ten or fifteen, families.

nese law and customs are observed. Japanese schools, hospitals, associations, and newspapers have been established, following the program set up by the emigration societies in Japan for the country of immigration. The national federation of Japanese emigration societies established in Brazil shops, warehouses and dwelling houses, sawmills, brick factories and hospitals. The building of new roads and bridges, surveying of new and unexploited tracts of land, etc., are also undertaken by the national federation.

Thus the Japanese immigrants in Brazil do not become *déracinés* but are under the constant influence of their native country. The emigration societies in Japan are the bridge between the old and the new fatherland.

Volume of Migration to Brazil

The only available statistical information concerning emigration from Japan is the record of passports issued and returned. The balance between the two figures is considered to represent the number of Japanese residing abroad. Hence, no data are published that take account of the natural increase of the Japanese population abroad. In the countries of Latin America, population censuses have been rare and inaccurate. For other reasons, too, it is not surprising that in the matter of Japanese residents the census figures often deviate from the corresponding figures published in Japan. For the sake of uniformity, therefore, and probably also that of probably greater accuracy, the Japanese figures have been primarily relied upon in the present study.

Table 5 indicates both the recentness of Japanese emigration to Latin America and the very small part which that to Spanish America has played since 1924 compared with that to Portuguese America.

TABLE 9. NATIONALITY OF IMMIGRANTS INTO BRAZIL, 1930 AND 1939

	1930	1939
Germans	4,180	1,975
Italians	4,253	1,004
Japanese	14,076	1,411
Poles	4,719	612
Portuguese	18,740	15,120

Source: Brazilian Ministry of Foreign Affairs, Rio de Janeiro, 1940.

TABLE 10. JAPANESE AND TOTAL NUMBER OF IMMIGRANTS INTO BRAZIL, 1933-1939

Year	Total	Japanese
1933	46,081	24,494
1934	46,027	21,930
1935	29,585	9,611
1936	12,733	3,306
1937	34,677	4,557
1938	19,388	2,524
1939	22,668	1,411

Source: *Revista de Imigração e Colonização*, Rio de Janeiro, October, 1940.

The statistics show an even more surprising trend, namely the almost complete transference of Japanese emigration since the United States exclusion law from Pacific to Atlantic destinations, that is, primarily from the United States and Canada to Brazil. A rather remarkable change in Japanese emigration policies is also reflected in the numbers of Japanese arrivals in Brazil, shown in Tables 9 and 10. Without seeking to find the explanations for minor fluctuations, we may recognize here the experimental nature of Japanese emigration to Brazil in the early years, the interruption during the two years of maximum German submarine activity, the effect of the earthquake in 1923, the rapid growth of the colonization program after the passage of the United States exclusion law, and the rapid diminution of that program with the continental expansion program in Asia after the occupation of Manchuria.

From the standpoint of the social and economic importance of Japanese immigration for Brazil, Table 10 is instructive. From it we see that from more than one-half of the total in 1933 it has declined to one-eighth in 1938 and one-sixteenth in 1939.

THE JAPANESE COLONIES IN BRAZIL

Latin American governments and economists have shown curiously little interest in their countrymen of Japanese origin. The literature is almost restricted to a few pamphlets dealing chiefly with racial or political aspects of Oriental immigration. Even the recent official investigation of the Japanese colonies in São Paulo has contributed little of value about their condition and functioning.

The total number of Japanese in Brazil at the present time is 240,000 to 300,000 according to various estimates, while the official Brazilian Federal figure is 186,-000. Private sources, as for instance the *Christian*

Science Monitor—usually well informed and careful in its statements—speak of about 500,000 foreign-born or first-generation Brazilian Japanese.[11] From well-informed Japanese-Brazilian sources, the present writer arrives at the conclusion that the total figure, including the natural increase, is not more than 230,000. There is no occasion for a separate estimate of the Japan-born and the Brazil-born, since almost all of the second generation retain their Japanese nationality. Of the total number of the Japanese only a few thousand (according to the *Christian Science Monitor* up to 20,000) live in the Northern states of Amazon and Pará, but the great majority are settled in Central Brazil, mostly in the state of São Paulo (about 200,000) and have spread over the borders of this state into the neighboring districts of the adjoining states of Minas Geraes, Matto Grosso, Paraná and Rio de Janeiro. Here is the old center of Japanese immigration.

In the state of São Paulo, besides Japanese settlements in Cotia, near to the capital, relatively small colonies along the Southern coast to the south of Santos and as far as Cananeia, mostly in the valley of Ribeira, there are three major sections grouped along the three railways—Noreste with its center in Aracatuba and Lins, the Alta-Paulista centered in Marilia and Bastos, and the Alta-Sorrocabana to the South of Campos Novos. In the neighboring state of Parana, Japanese settlements have been established in the municipalities of Cornelio Procopio, Londrina and S. Jeronimo.

The Japanese own approximately 1,250,000 acres of

[11] See the issue of March 25, 1942.

land in the state of São Paulo alone—an area about the size of the state of Delaware. While others are interesting as indications of a trend to expand and also perhaps from a strategical standpoint, economically only the settlements in the state of São Paulo are of importance. In the outskirts of the Federal capital, Rio de Janeiro, much truck farming land is worked by Japanese.

Organization of Settlements

As has already been stated, the Japanese settlements in central Brazil were organized by the Kaigai Kogyo Kabushiki Kaisha, but a few small "independent" colonies exist in São Paulo as well as in the state of Rio de Janeiro. Typical for these smaller colonies is that organized by the Japanese newspaper concern, the *Osaka Mainichi*. The Kaigai Kogyo Kaisha has offices in almost all parts of Latin America, but the center of its activity is in Central Brazil.

The first Japanese colony was established in Iguapé (state of São Paulo) in 1912. The emigration began with contract laborers, as the local coffee industry suffers from a constant shortage of labor. The situation was similar to that of Hawaii where the sugar producers at that time were also anxious to get Japanese laborers. The Japanese policy, after 1924, of transforming the laborers into settlers, met with remarkable success in this part of Brazil. Most of the Japanese in this region are engaged in agriculture: as coffee plantation laborers, semi-independent farmers, and independent farmers. The activity of the farmers is not limited to coffee. The rice crop in Brazil increased under Japanese influence from 688,000 tons in 1926 to 1,502,220 tons in 1939. Of this figure more than one-third is the share of the state of São Paulo. The Japanese began to cultivate sugar and cotton. The cultivation of tea made remarkable progress in Iguapé (São Paulo) and on a smaller scale in other colonies. Starting from zero, the Japanese created a silk industry in Brazil. There are at present in São Paulo more than 15,000 mulberry trees, and Brazil no longer imports silk. A large percentage of banana plantations as well as vegetable and truck gardens and fishing in São Paulo are in Japanese hands.

The Japan Cotton Trading Company is engaged not only in cotton trade with the North of Brazil but also in the silk industry; and it is pioneering in tea culture. The Japanese colonies possess their own rice mills, lumber mills, sugar factory, mandioca mills, and an electric power station. The Kaigai Kogyo Kaisha is the chief Japanese entrepreneur in Central Brazil. The company selects, purchases and sells land, finances these transactions, is engaged in warehousing, engineering, trading, banking, agriculture, fishing, and mining. Whereas between 1932 and 1934 the Japanese farmers raised 5 per cent of the coffee and 8 per cent of the rice —both long-established crops in this state—they dominated the new crops that have been started more recently. They produced 46 per cent of the cotton, 57 per cent of the silk, and 75 per cent of the tea. Although the Japanese make up only 2 to 3 per cent of the total population of São Paulo and only 5 per cent of the landowners, occupying only 1.77 per cent of the agricultural land, they account for 29.5 per cent of the agricultural production.[12] According to Japanese-Brazilian sources 90 per cent are active in agriculture. They control a substantial part of the food supply of the city of São Paulo.

The entire economic and social life of almost all Japanese immigrants in Central Brazil is regulated, directed, and supervised by the Kaigai Kogyo Kaisha.

The Brazil Takushoku Kumai also has expanded its land acquisitions in Central Brazil. This organization purchased in 1931 around 650,000 acres and originated six settlements, the Bastos, the Tiete, the Alliance, the Villa Nova, the Tres Barros, and the Suassuhy Grand. Of these the first two are the most important. All of them are small, independent technically up-to-date economic units with centralized management of plantations, several industrial enterprises, and conveniences rare in new colonies in Brazil.

Principal Economic Activities

The Japanese live almost completely isolated from the native element in Brazil. The population of their centers varies from three hundred to six or seven thousand, in cities, towns, and large *fazendas,* but always they remain in atmosphere and surroundings completely Japanese. Typical is one of the oldest Japanese settlements in Brazil, that in the town of Registro (formerly Colonia Japoneza) in the hot, moist, coastal region of the state of São Paulo, southwest of Santos.

[12] Preston E. James, in the *Geographical Review,* January, 1937, pp. 145-146.

The buildings, the fields, the crops have all been reproduced from those of Japan—only the background is different; and while in Japan about 90 per cent of the holdings are less than 2 hectares in size, in Registro the average is about 25 hectares. In Registro, a city of nine thousand population, about six thousand are Japanese. Of 45 business firms only a few are Brazilian. Japanese laborers, storekeepers, drivers, schools with only Japanese students make it a piece of Japan in Brazil—even the Buddhist temples are not missing. The Japanese supervising company imports Japanese products, medicines, school books, and employs Japanese doctors and dentists. Local Japanese cooperatives embrace all the colony's trade and are, like the colonization companies, under complete supervision and management by officials appointed from Tokyo.

More recently the Japanese cooperatives in the state of São Paulo specialized in constructing bridges, roads, waterworks, plants. The nine purely agricultural cooperatives, according to 1942 data, controlled one-fifth of the São Paulo cotton crop and almost all the crops of potato and truck gardens.

The more recent Japanese colonization in the North of Brazil is of a different character. Its territorial size is substantially larger: on both sides of the Amazon river the Japanese own more than six million acres of land (equal in area to the state of Maryland). These immense territories have been obtained by the Japanese as concessions from the states of Pará and Amazon.

The leader in Pará is the South American Developing Company (Nambei Takushoku Kaisha), organized in Tokyo in 1923 with a large initial capital contributed by the Bank of Japan, the big commercial banks, trading and shipping concerns, and some cities. The majority owner and head of this enterprise is the Japanese textile concern Kanegafuchi, belonging to the Mitsui group. After visits made by several Japanese missions representing commerce, industry and science, and after a study of the best location available for the concession, land was selected on the rivers Acara and Guama, and an option on these lands amounting to 2,500,000 acres in three lots was obtained for two years. At the same time, agricultural lands were secured also along the Braganca railway in the district of Castanhal.

The Japanese made use of the option and formed the Companhia Nipponica de Plantação do Brasil, S. A., of which the energetic Hashiro Fukuhara became the manager. Brazilian capitalists from Rio de Janeiro joined the Japanese group. This concession, in spite of the lapse of many years, is still in an experimental stage, but development has begun in Acara. The administrative center is in Thomeasú, about eleven hours by riverboat from the port of Belém (Pará.) The Japanese have erected there modern buildings, storehouses, radio stations. The company declared its intention to grow cacao, cotton, and rice, and to transplant every year several hundred Japanese families. Although the enterprise was still in the experimental stage, 1500 Japanese, representing 227 families, were already living in these colonies in 1934.[13] According to more

[13] Directoria Geral da Agricultura, Industria e Comercio, Belém—letter of March 21, 1934.

recent reports, numerous individual houses and even some apartment buildings have been erected. Rice, corn, sweet potatoes, vegetables, and tropical fruits are being raised by the colonists, vegetables being sent down the river to Belém, the capital of the state. Two schools have been established with an enrollment of more than two hundred children.

Since 1930, the Japanese capitalist, Tsukasa Myetsuka, has held another large concession in the State of Amazon (Amazon Development Company). This concession lies near Parantins, about eight hundred miles upstream on the north bank of the Amazon, about 150 miles east of the Ford rubber plantations. Like the Kanegafuchi group, the Myetsuka concern entered as a pioneer in a wilderness. Future colonies in this case were planned on an even larger scale. An Amazonia Institute has been established in Tokyo to train leaders for this type of colonization. This institute, to begin with, sent two hundred graduates to Brazil to complete further studies in an "Agro-Industrial Institute" at Paratina, also launched by Myetsuka. Their first step was the establishment of Acaka, an experimental colony, headed by agricultural engineers who had studied soil and weather conditions and the best types of activity suited to the country. This model colony is supposed to serve as an example for future colonization. According to Dr. Henrique Bahiano, representative of the Brazilian Ministry of Agriculture, who visited Tokyo, the Myetsuka enterprise hoped to send settlers in large numbers.

No definite plans are known about the activity of

these enterprises. There were rumors at one time that the Myetsuka group intended to cultivate rubber and the Kanegafuchi concern—cotton. The Japanese have already had experience with rubber, as rubber has been produced under Japanese management in British Malaya and the East Indies, extending to Java, Sumatra and Borneo. (These enterprises are financially supported by the Oriental Development Company, the Taiwan Bank, and others). On the other hand, there are indications that these groups really intended to develop a process of polyculture. Experiments have been made with rice, jute, white pepper.

Emigration as Part of Capitalistic Expansion

If we compare the two types of the Japanese penetration in Brazil—in Central Brazil and in the north—while both of them are strictly planned, organized and regulated, we notice an important distinction: In the case of the colonies in Central Brazil the human migration is important, but it is organized and accompanied by capital investments of the Kaigai Kogyo Kaisha. The North Brazilian concessions of the Japanese, on the other hand, are a phenomenon, chiefly, not of human but of capital migration and preliminary investigation. They recall the French Sociétés des Etudes. It is a case of export of capital to Brazil, or preparation for such export, only incidentally accompanied by its national representatives. It is an overseas extension of the concerns of Kanegafuchi and Myetsuka. It is a phenomenon in the same category as the setting up of foreign-owned factories in China or India. It is a case of expansion comparable with that of the United States "Big 30" described by the writer in his *Struggle for South America*.[14] It takes the form of export of capital as preparation for large-scale emigration.

The Kaigai Kogyo Kaisha functions in the most thickly populated and most highly cultivated part of Brazil and does not make such long-term plans as the Northern concessionaires who are truly pioneers in the wilderness. Perhaps the Japanese concerns are primarily pursuing their effort to secure sources of raw material—the extension of cotton or rubber cultures in the style of Ford concessions in Amazon or Firestone's in Liberia—but their secret and open desires do not change the general picture of a highly centralized planning and financing of emigration.

This characteristic can be traced even in the small independent colonies, like that of the newspaper *Osaka Mainichi,* where the colonists are obliged to invest their savings in Japanese enterprises in Brazil and are not allowed to return with their savings to Japan.

Japanese penetration of Portuguese America is supported by the Japanese banks of which the Bank of Taiwan, itself of colonial origin in Formosa, is especially active, having an organized net of correspondents all over the Atlantic coast of Latin America. The Yokohama Specie Bank has a branch in Rio de Janeiro and concentrates on transactions with Japan aside from its large local business.

The general character of the emigration to Brazil is, in short, a part of Japanese-managed economy. The

[14] London-New York, 1931.

former Japanese Ambassador to Brazil, Mr. Akika Akiyoshi, expressed this policy in August 1930:

"The development of emigration to Brazil requires, under any circumstances, courageous advances by our capitalists. One can only view with pleasure a movement of our capitalists toward South America such as we have witnessed lately, since that is an essential prerequisite for emigration to Brazil."

The idea of this form of emigration is not new in Japan. As early as 1913, Dr. Ishihashi, in speaking of Mexico, said:

"There is a good deal of talk of Japanese capitalistic colonization and enterprises in that country. But so far nothing has appeared in a tangible form and the reason for this appears to be the fact that Japan is not yet in a financial position to undertake such enterprises even if possible."[15]

When the time was ripe for this kind of enterprise Japan preferred to start it in Portuguese America. The earthquake of 1923, the Exclusion Act of 1924 in the United States, and an analogous policy in all English-speaking countries on the Pacific and in some of the Spanish American countries forced the Japanese Government to reconsider its emigration policy. The method of elimination directed attention to Brazil. Japan's land hunger coincided with Brazil's population hunger. Even when the Japanese Food-Population Commission of 1928 decided that the solution of Japan's population problem lay not in emigration but

[15] *Op. cit.*, p. 123.

in industrialization, the interest in Brazil as an eventual outlet for a part of the yearly unemployed labor surplus remained unchanged, probably strengthened by political and strategical considerations.

The financial feature of Japanese emigration is limited to the recent movement to Brazil. We do not find it in Japanese emigration to Spanish America, although the organized character of Japanese emigration in a milder form and on a smaller scale can be traced there also in the last ten or twelve years.

Japanese settlement in the northern part of the country was economically welcome in Brazil, not because of the Japanese investments (their amount could not compete with those of Europe and the United States), but because workers equipped with capital and modern technique furnished the best possible means of moving the economic frontier of Brazil. Brazilian economic history shows a constant movement of that frontier within the political limits of the federation from the coast into the interior. States like Amazon, Matto Grosso and Pará are, from an economic standpoint, still undeveloped colonies of coastal Brazil.[16]

While Japanese immigration in Central Brazil contributed to the solution of the labor problem, in the north, Japanese colonization meant the movement of the economic frontier on a large, planned scale, with modern techniques.

A speech by the President of Brazil, Dr. Getulio Vargas, on a visit to the State of Pará confirms this interpretation:

[16] J. F. Normano, *Brazil. A Study of Economic Types*, Chapel Hill, 1935.

"Experiments of Henry Ford with rubber and lumber, and of Japanese colonists with diversified agriculture, foreshadow a bright future for the almost empty Amazon Basin.

"I like to imagine what this region, unequalled in area, will be like when in it are fixed the intelligence and activity of 100,000,000 Brazilians. . . .

"The Americans have transformed the inhospitable forest into a promising agricultural and industrial center. They plant rationally to harvest and industrialize. They substitute, for a primitive extractive system, an agricultural industry, and thus show the way to economic possibilities of Amazonia.

"The Japanese, in a different manner, form small colonization groups which devote themselves to agriculture, with hygienic and technical assistance. The process of polyculture they have adopted is succeeding."

Even the small influx of Japanese capital has been considered very favorably in Brazil, especially in the early thirties when foreign investments from other countries stopped, when gold reserves were used to pay foreign debt obligations, and difficulties with foreign exchange began. From the technical standpoint of the Brazilian balance of payments, every kind and size of capital import gave temporary relief.

Popular Attitudes toward Japanese Immigration

The Japanese policy in Brazil carefully avoided possibilities of conflict. The unorganized Japanese emigration in some parts of Spanish America (especially in Peru) soon added to the number of shopkeepers and traders whose occupations were competitive with those of the natives. In Brazil this kind of urbanized Japanese is less in evidence. The immigrants have their roots in the soil and are engaged mostly in agriculture. According to the population census of the Japanese residents abroad in 1930, the chief occupations of the Japanese living in Latin America were commerce in Mexico, agriculture and commerce in Cuba, commerce in Panama, Colombia, and Venezuela, commerce in Bolivia, commerce in Chile, industry, commerce and agriculture in Argentina, agriculture in Brazil.[17]

In the eyes of the mass of the population in Brazil, the Japanese for a large period of time represented a respectable organized economic power directed toward the economic welfare of the country. The people in Spanish America, on the other hand, considered them as petty traders and in general still do not distinguish the Japanese petty trader from the Chinese. The Pacific coast of the American continent became acquainted with all types of Japanese emigrants—schoolboys, *dekasegi* ("birds of passage"), semi-privately organized contract laborers, semi-privately organized colonists. In Brazil the Japanese made a fresh start with new methods: there they sent only the settler and the capitalist. Even the contract laborers received no promise of return passage; they were expected to settle in the country. The experience on the Pacific coast, especially in the English-speaking countries, influenced this new policy. The United States and Canada asked for cheap labor and received competitors; a rivalry of interests intensified by racial difference was bound to develop.

[17] For details of the occupations followed by Japanese residents in the various countries of Latin America see Table 6.

Japan decided to avoid this conflict on the Atlantic coast.

Even the sex distribution of the Japanese in Brazil shows this steady character of their immigration in Brazil in comparison with that in other countries of the American continent. As will be seen from Table 2 on page 11, women followed the Japanese emigrants from the time of their first appearance in Brazil. Japanese immigration in Brazil has never been almost womanless as was the case in some periods in Spanish America. For the early stages the year 1913 is typical: in Mexico and Peru 95 per cent of the Japanese immigrants were male; in Brazil, only 60 per cent.

Thus both economic and social motives explain clearly the former favorable attitude of Brazil toward Japanese penetration. An inquiry undertaken in the state of São Paulo among various classes of the people resulted in replies of which 75 per cent were favorable to the Japanese. In March, 1934, the Directoria Geral da Agricultura, Industria e Comercio in Belém informed the writer to the same effect. The new Japanese emigration policy proved to be in harmony with the requirements of the local environment.

We can see what Japanese immigration means to São Paulo from the following episode during the last outbreak of revolt in São Paulo in 1932. The port Santos had been under blockade by the Federal Government when the Japanese steamer Buenos Aires Maru arrived with Japanese immigrants. The Brazilian naval blockade was momentarily suspended to allow a shipload of immigrants to land. Both federal and

Paulista authorities were waiting to receive them; by contract they were destined for Santos in the State of São Paulo, to which it would have been expensive for the Government to transport them by railroad from Rio de Janeiro; so revolutionary operations were interrupted, and a fleeting truce was arranged to allow the transport ship to touch at a small island outside the port of Santos, where the immigrants could be landed and conveyed to the mainland by launch. This was very much of an exception to the rule. The blockade of Santos had been strict; no other vessels had been allowed to enter.

A Brazilian survey of Japanese colonies in São Paulo in 1933 confirms the existence of this attitude. Fernando Callage who visited the colonies commends the selection and preparation of the Japanese emigrants. He refers to statements by local authorities that "the Japanese *colono* is the best factor of progress for local life," and describes the full harmony existing between the Japanese and natives. His conclusions are that the Japanese is "a *colono* of great efficiency, hard working, orderly, economical, obedient and law-abiding... The Japanese as owner of a coffee plantation (there are hundreds of them in the state) takes his place by the side of our best agriculturists. Japanese effort on the plantations which we visited is outstanding."[18] Callage does not neglect to mention the discontent in São Paulo about cases of urbanization of immigrants and their occupation as storekeepers and petty traders. The

[18] "As Colonias Japonesas de São Paulo," in *Boletim do Departamento do Trabolho Agricola*, São Paulo, 1933.

size of Japanese investments in Brazil, or in Latin America as a whole, there is reason to believe that even in 1931, when many of the more important settlement projects were as yet incipient, those in North Brazil alone exceeded fifty million yen. During the decade, an offer of Japanese financiers to participate in Brazilian shipping was favorably considered by the Conselho Federal de Comercio. Japanese concerns also negotiated for concessions of Brazilian nickel deposits in the state of Goyaz.

The economic character of the relations between Japan and Brazil calls for emphasis. There were no political sympathies with Japan in Portuguese America comparable with those in Spanish America. Distrust of the "colossus of the north," the *peligro yanqui*, in the latter sometimes led to a political current in favor of an eventual military alliance with Japan against the United States. Brazil never played with the idea of a racial kinship between its pre-Columbian population and that of Japan. In fact, the *peligro yanqui* feeling did not exist in Brazil which never has had a serious conflict with the United States and is traditionally friendly in its attitude to the northern republic.[20] Nor was Brazil an active party to the triangular relations which for some time existed between the United States, Japan, and Latin America. Nevertheless, Japanese-Brazilian relations have in some cases been subject to propaganda. Importers to Japan of Brazilian coffee have opened in Tokyo and in Osaka coffee houses

---

[20] Cf. J. F. Normano, *Struggle for South America*, op. cit., and "Changing Latin American Attitudes" in *Foreign Affairs*, October 1932.

as the feud between the two great ancient Japanese families, the Taira and the Minamoto. Unfortunately, the investigators did not pay attention to possible social dangers in the Japanese settlements in the region, but they did arrive at the general conclusion that the Japanese nuclei resist any tendency to assimilate to the Brazilian milieu.

The stubborn *Kulturkampf* organized by the Japanese in connection with the recently announced Brazilian requirements of education in Portuguese shows how deeply Japanese these colonists feel. Despite strict police measures they continue their clandestine Japanese schools. They use illegal textbooks in Japanese which, according to the statements of some independent witnesses, contain subversive propaganda as well as technical military instruction.

TRADE AND INVESTMENT

Table 8 on p. 16 shows that between 1931 and 1939 the trade between Japan and Brazil has become by far the most important of those with Latin American countries. Whereas in the former year, Brazil came in fifth place as a Latin American importer of Japanese products and in fourth place as a source of supply for Japan, it dominated both aspects of this foreign trade in 1939. And this happened despite the fact that Japanese cotton growing in São Paulo supplied to an ever increasing extent a raw material for Brazilian manufacture in competition with one of Japan's most important export industries.

While estimates vary considerably as regards the

report states that the population of the settlement is predominantly Japanese, about 90 per cent, organized by the Kaigai Kogyo Kabushiki Kaisha, and administrated in Brazil partly through its subsidiary the Sociedade Colonisadora do Brazil (Bratac). The investigators confirm the agricultural character of the Japanese immigrants and admire their spirit of organization which they consider an expression of the general character of the planned and managed Japanese emigration system.

The entire direction and administration of all activities in Bastos is concentrated in the Bratac whose office is a nerve center of the region. The office employs some Brazilians, the most important among them being a legal adviser. In adition to the planned polycultural activities (coffee and cotton as the main crops), there are a silk factory (100 workers), a flour mill, and twelve small plants for various manufactures. The report praises the sanitary improvements and sanitary condition of the settlement. The investigators seem to be surprised that all signs and inscriptions are in Japanese, that in the offices of the Bratac no books can be found in any other language than Japanese, that all the technical manuals are in Japanese, that the only book in Portuguese they encountered in the two libraries was a *Dicionario Pratico Ilustrado,* and that even a Portuguese-Japanese dictionary could not be found while it was supposed to exist. The report emphasized that all books and periodicals in the settlement are in Japanese, even the children's literature which includes stories of purely Japanese interest, such

presence of Japanese in non-agricultural occupations is resented in Brazil not less than in Spanish America. A comparison of the Japanese immigration to Brazil and to Spanish America shows that group action and capital investment are responsible for the economic success in Brazil. The most peculiar features of the Japanese penetration in Brazil are the speed of the movement, the dynamics of its development, and its novel character. But now in 1942, it is a closed chapter the continuing economic influence and importance of which have not yet been investigated. Political events have compelled the Brazilians and the Brazilian Government to revise their attitude toward Japanese immigration and to consider its eventual political and strategical danger while admitting its favorable economic influence. In addition to measures intended to prevent a further increase of Japanese residents in Brazil, the Government has decided upon a strict control of existing colonies.

The Brazilian Conselho de Imigração e Colonização which since 1938 exercises this supervision published in 1941 the results of a field study of some of the Japanese colonies.[19] It should be noted that one of the investigators, Aristoteles de Lima Camara (the second vice-president of the Board), was the representative of the General Staff of the Army. They choose Bastos (in the municipality of Tupan, in the valley of the River Peixe, along the Noroeste R.R.) as a representative Japanese settlement in the state of São Paulo. The

[19] "Colonizacoes Niponica e Germanica no Sul do Brasil," *Revista de Imigração e Colonização*, Rio de Janeiro, January, 1941.

decorated with murals which do not fail to make the most of Japanese participation in the production of that commodity. Brazil also for some time supported a commercial museum in Yokohama. Moreover, there was organized by Brazilian diplomats the *Correio da Asia*, in which Brazilian and Japanese economists collaborated. One of its publications was introduced by Dr. P. Leão Velloso, at the time ambassador in Tokyo, who emphasized the identity of his views with those of the founder, Consul Raul Bopp, and of his successor, a Dr. José Jobim. The books published by the Brazilian organization in Japan deal with Brazilian subjects but disclose the influence of Japanese residence and contacts. The sources of information in many instances are Japanese.

While a larger program of studies and publications in Japan did not materialize, there was established in Rio de Janeiro in 1939 a Centro de Estudos Economicos, connected with the Foreign Office and with the Federal Trade Council, in which the original founders continued the work originally set up with Japanese collaborators in Yokohama. The "inestimable collaboration" of these associates is, indeed, acknowledged. Several of these had moved to Rio.

As recently as June 26, 1940, the Minister of Foreign Affairs signed a foreword to one of the center's publications, in which he referred to war conditions and made favorable mention of the editor, Consul José Jobim. Raul Bopp, the founder (more recently consul in California), is well known, among other things, for having at times publicly protested against restrictions of Japanese immigration and colonization, as evidences of a short-sighted view.

WAR AND THE FUTURE

We are thus brought to the consideration of an aspect of Japanese colonization in Brazil that may have escaped those students who have considered that subject exclusively from an economic standpoint. To what extent was the Japanese trade drive in Latin America, and more in particular the minutely planned combination of industrial investments and colonization in Brazil, part of a program of war preparation?

Remembering the activity of Japanese colonists in the Philippines, and in the Netherlands East Indies, it may be well to examine the geographical location of the Japanese settlements in Brazil. They are situated along the lines of a crescent which starts from the highly industrialized city of São Paulo in the south, swings west and north through Matto Grosso and the Amazon Valley, then eastward to the Atlantic Coast province of Ceara. Most of it lies in the state of São Paulo, probably the most industrialized part of Latin America. About two hundred thousand well organized nationalistic Japanese, used to group work, severely resisting any attempts to assimilate them, trained in Japan for Brazil and in Brazil for Japan, may well have been intended to fulfill other than purely economic functions in the interest of their homeland. Their extension on the coast where they meet the German colonies in the South, their extension to Minas Geraes, the presence of large Italian and German groups in

THE JAPANESE IN BRAZIL 57

São Paulo, the Japanese territorial proximity to industrial plants in São Paulo and Rio de Janeiro, and to the mineral wealth of Minas Geraes—all this may have been more than mere accident. The immense Japanese concessions in the unexplored Amazon region may have been intended as a springboard for aggression by air in many directions. The President of Brazil, Getulio Vargas, at the time of his visit to the Amazon region in 1940 emphasized its continental character, its importance for the defense of the continent, and intended to bring together in a conference the nations touching on the Amazon Valley region—Peru, Ecuador, Colombia, Bolivia, Brazil. This plan was not carried out, however. We do not know (the Brazilians do not know either) the exact number of Japanese residing in this region, but the Japanese certainly have had a good chance and enough time to get acquainted with the jungles of that region.[21]

POSTSCRIPT

Most of the preceding pages were written prior to Brazil's entrance into the war. The stormy public opinion and the street demonstrations in favor of the war caused President Vargas to make the decisive move in spite of a certain lack of sympathy in some governmental circles toward the break with the Axis. The war declaration brought with it at first a hysterical search for fifth columnists, with special attention given to the Japanese as the most conspicuous, though smaller and internally less influential than the strong German

[21] See Earl Parker Hanson's article in the *New York Herald Tribune*, February 22, 1942.

groups. The press began its revelations of plots organized by the Japanese colonists in São Paulo. Wide publicity was given to the alleged admission by some Japanese in São Paulo of the existence of an extended, well prepared subversive plan. Japanese spies were arrested and equipment was seized. Reports were released that Japanese groups in the State of São Paulo own heavy artillery and automatic arms, and are prepared to assault military bases, seize factories and railways, and cut communications on the main strategic points. The press claimed that the port of Santos already was largely surrounded by a ring of Japanese. The police discovered Japanese agents as well as military and naval officers among the humble and industrious settlers. It was made public that Japanese fishermen in the vicinity of the naval center of Ilha Grande, between Rio de Janeiro and Santos, in some cases held commissions in the Japanese Navy.

It is difficult to confirm or to deny all these revelations and allegations: but the Brazilian authorities certainly have shown themselves persistent and systematic in their watchful activity. From the strategical standpoint, the United Nations were pleased by Brazil's action in view of the strategic importance of Natal on the "bulge" of Brazil, separated only by 1700 miles from Africa. But it is not yet entirely clear whether the United Nations, including Brazil, have given sufficient attention to the existence of Japanese groups in the Amazon region which is not only important strategically but also a large potential arsenal of raw materials.

Part II

THE JAPANESE IN PERU
By Antonello Gerbi

I. THE PAST

Early Contacts

The theory that the Incas originally came from Japan is of course without foundation, but not without significance. It seeks to establish a racial origin which would gratify some Peruvians and at the same time prevent any discrimination on nationalistic grounds. Moreover, since in Peru rightist elements are overwhelmingly Spanish-conscious, whereas leftist sympathizers are inclined to stress the indigenous elements of their society, the theory of the Incas' Japanese origin had all the virtue of appealing to these latter groups, which are the most apt of any to be politically prejudiced against the Japanese.

Like the Negro slaves and Chinese before them, Japanese were encouraged to migrate to Peru by coastal landowners, most of whom were conservative, of Spanish descent and afflicted with a chronic labor shortage. Therefore the Japanese were hated by poor natives who considered them to be cheap and hence dangerous competitors. These native laborers were almost all *mestizos*—there are few pure-blooded Indians on the coast—and they regarded the Japanese as an inferior race. If it could be established that the latter were related to the old ruling Peruvian class, then even *mestizos* would have to show them more consideration. It is well known that racial pride in Inca descent is much stronger among *mestizos* than among pure-bred Indios. "The Indians of the highlands . . . have lost much if not all their racial self-respect. It is the educated *mestizos* . . . who . . .take pride in the achievements of the Incas."[1] Therefore the theory held a doubtful appeal for coastal Peruvians, which goes far to explain why it was not more widely accepted..

This theory was perhaps first formulated, toward the end of the 18th century, in an essay by Bernardin de Saint-Pierre. After mentioning the attraction which the Rising Sun exercised on ancient peoples, he wrote: "It was through this attraction that the peoples of Asia, moving from one island to the next, arrived in the New World, where they landed on the coast of Peru. They brought with them the names of the children of the sun which they were seeking."[2]

This hypothesis was supported and developed by

[1] Bingham, H., *Inca Land, Explorations in the Highlands of Peru*, Boston and New York, 1922, p. 258. The situation has now altered somewhat through the efforts of the *Indigenistas*. But Bingham's assertion is still true in the main, and it was even truer when the Inca-descent theory was first put forward.

[2] *Etudes de la nature*, 1784, Etude XI, Paris, n.d., p. 355. A few years later Humboldt indicated several affinities between Japanese and Peruvian or Mexican civilization (see, e.g., *Vues des Cordillères et monuments des peuples indigènes de l'Amérique*, n.d. (1816?), I, pp. 39, 343, 384-5). The common symbol of the sun was perhaps responsible for recent rumors that Japanese officers fought with Peruvian troops. In a Guayaquil newspaper it was reported that the Peruvian forces display the Japanese sun on their helmets. "Ese Sol," a Peruvian general promptly replied, "no es el 'Sol Naciente' de los Nipones. Es el 'Sol de los Incas' " (Ballesteros, E. F., in a letter to *El Telégrafo, Guayaquil*, March 18, 1911, quoted in *El Universal*, Lima, March 19, 1941).

Francisco A. Loayza, a Peruvian *mestizo* with a Spanish name (a Loayza was the first Archbishop of Lima), who, after ten years in Japan (1912-22), concluded that Manko Kapac, the founder of the Inca Empire, had been a Japanese. Loayza sustained this thesis at the Twenty-second International Congress of Americanists in Rome. Most, but not all, of his arguments were philological and etymological.[3] He regarded the institution of *Amautas* (Inca sages and teachers) as typically Japanese.[4] He described how the Japanese managed to reach the Peruvian coast. Following the Kuro-Sivo Current, Manko landed in Arica Bay, turned around, and then climbed to the Morro, which was to become famous later during the Pacific War through the heroic sacrifice of Colonel Ugarte. After he had seen some of the poor natives, "the altruistic spirit of Manko Kapac assumed the philanthropic duty of civilizing them. And he devised the glorious program of his apostolic and

[3] He declared that the words *Manko Kapac, Titicaca, Inka, Cuzco, Yawar Waka, Mama Occlo, Koya, Kon Tecsi* are "perfectamente japonesas" (Loayza, Fr. A., *Manko Kapac, El fundador del Imperio de los Inkas fué japonés, Para,* 1926, pp. 67, 71-9); that the *Yaravi* are Japanese (p. 92); and that in general, "Es asombrosa la integridad que conservaron las palabras japonesas a través de los siglos, en la nueva patria de los Inkas" (p. 91). As proof he announced the publication of a *Vocabulario Misterioso* with more than 200 Japanese and Inca words (p. 97). Loayza remembered that an Argentine, Alejandro Gancedo, held "que el idioma kechua, en su origen, fué el japonés adulterado" (*Revista de Derecho, Historia y Letras,* Buenos Aires, Sept. 1922), but in his opinion the Kechuas were indigenous, and only the Incas came from Japan. The Loayza book was praised and his theory accepted by the Cuban jurist Dr. F. Carrera Justiz. See his leaflet *Era Japonés Manko-Capa, Fundador del Imperia Inca en el Perú* (El Urbanismo Prehistórico en el Cuzco), Habana, 1940, p. 28. For similar theories, see the bibliography in Pericot y Garcia, *La América Indígena,* Barcelona, 1936, pp. 380-1, 422, 140 n.

[4] "Nada prueba tanto la procedencia japonesa de los Inkas que la sabia Institución de los Amautas" (Loayza, *Manka Kapac,* cit., p. 88).

constructive mission . . ."[5] Why or when Manko Kapac left Japan for South America is not made clear. Loayza reserved the solution of this problem for a subsequent book, *El Parentesco de dos pueblos*.[6] But it is clear that he thinks the expedition was deliberate, not accidental, in contrast to the theory expounded a century earlier about the arrival on the Peruvian coast of a Mongol expedition which had been bound for Japan and had suffered dispersal by a storm.[7] The Japanese, too, have utilized the Manko Kapac legend. It is said that the story is taught in Japanese schools.[8] Moreover, in all Lima there is only one monument to an "indigenous personality," as a local guidebook puts it,[9] and that is the statue of Manko Kapac,

[5] "El espíritu altruista de Manko Kapac se impuso al compasivo deber de civilizarlas [las gentes indígenas]. Y trazó el programa glorioso de su mision apostólica y constructiva . . . ." (*ibid.*, p. 111).
[6] This book was never published. In a letter of December 15, 1939 to Professor Carrera Justiz and quoted by him in his *Era Japonés Manko-Capa* (p. 8, n. 1) the date of the arrival of the Japanese on the Peruvian coast is provisionally fixed as the 13th century!
[7] "En 1829 [?] John Ranking supuso que una expedición de Kublai-Kan que se dirigía al Japón fué dispersada por un temporal, llegaron las naves a Sudamérica y fundaron al reino del Perú" (Pericot y Garcia, *cit.*, p. 380: Ranking, J., *Historical Researches on the Conquest of Peru, Mexico . . . by the Mongols with Elephants*, London, 1827 (?), suppl. 1834). Gornes MacPherson, M.J., *Sangre de Asia en América*, Caracas, 1939, states with very slight justification that Chinese "fueron los primeros en llegar a tierra americana" (p. 12), and that the Inca civilization was of Chinese origin (pp. 60-4).
[8] According to Guevara, Victor J., *Las Grandes Cuestiones Nacionales*, Cuzo, 1939, p. 156. Carleton Beals writes: "The Incas, they [the Japanese] declare, are really Oriental people; their ancestors came from Japan and Manchuria." (*America South*, New York, 1938, pp. 444-5).
[9] *Guía Azul*, Lima, 1940 (?), p. 136. Apropos of statues, Upton Close (*Le Peril Japonais*, Paris, 1936, p. 456, quoted in de Lauwe, *l'Amérique Ibérique*, Paris, 1937, p. 208) gives the erroneous impression that Peru possesses a monument to Japanese heroes. "Au Pérou, la communauté japonaise achète des avions et érige des statues aux héros de Changhai." Of course, there are no such statues. The Japanese colony in Peru did

which was given by the Japanese colony in Peru on the occasion of the hundredth anniversary of Peruvian independence (1821-1921).[10]

The possible artistic influence of Japanese sculptors and wood-carvers during the Spanish Colonial period also belongs to the prehistorical epoch, at least as far as economic relations are concerned. It has been stated authoritatively that Franciscan missionaries, sent from Mexico to Japan, brought back converted Japanese artists, whose influence is traceable in the churches and their altar decorations all along the Pacific coast, and especially in Quito and Lima.[11] Some Oriental artefacts, too, arrived in Lima, probably via Acapulco.

But there was no real commerce, nor even lasting cultural intercourse. Abbé de Pauw, a popular French writer of the second half of the 18th century, noted this lack. "The Asiatics have been so stupidly indifferent to the news of the discovery of another hemisphere that they have never sent a ship thither. The Japanese ... who could have voyaged to the Western hemisphere

---

send money to Japan to help defray the cost of erecting a monument in Tokyo, near the Seishoji Shrine, to the memory of three famous "human bombs" who had sacrificed themselves in the Battle of Shanghai. See Close, *op. cit.*, p. 380; Zischka, Antoine, *Le Japon dans le monde*, Paris, 1935, p. 94. For a picture of the monument, see *ibid.*, pp. 192-3.

[10] Possibly as a reciprocal courtesy, one of the best-known Peruvian rightists, Sr. de la Riva Aguero, offered to give the Zoological Gardens in Tokyo three female vicuñas, the sacred animal of the Incas.

[11] The "Orientalistic" theory about the origins of Spanish Colonial art was supported by the Italian G. A. Sartorio, the Ecuadorean José Gabriel Navarro, and the Argentine Martin J. Noel. But it was vigorously attacked by the Peruvian Santiago Antunez de Mayolo, *Lima Precolombiana y Virreynal*, Lima, 1938, pp. 205, 208, 209-24.

by the way of the South Seas, as the Manila galleons did, have steadfastly refused to do so."[12]

Developments Before 1914

Peru was the first among South American countries to establish diplomatic relations with the Japanese Empire (1873). The instructions given to the Peruvian agent sent to Tokyo stressed, among other things, the importance of establishing cordial relations with countries which, through the export of goods and the emigration of their inhabitants, were in a position to assist in the development of Peruvian agriculture. The agent had instructions to guarantee good living conditions in Peru to immigrants from China and Japan.[13] Yet the treaty signed in Tokyo on August 21, 1873,[14] did not result in any emigration during the next 25 years. Even trade remained practically non-existent.

Active economic relations between Peru and Japan may be said to have begun as late as 1897. In that year, for the first time, steps were taken to secure an organized group of Japanese as immigrants to Peru. These

---

[12] De Pauw, Corneille, *Recherches Philosophiques sur les Américains, ou mémoires intéressants pour servir a l'Histoire de l'Espèce Humaine*, Berlin, 1768-9, II, p. 189. The same astonishment over this deviation from the "cours normal du developpement naval" has been expressed recently by Close, *op. cit.*, pp. 67-8.

[13] Lembcke, Jorge Bailey, "La Primera Misión Diplomática del Perú en el Japon," *El Comercio*, October 26, 1941. It is possible that the *Maria Luz* incident in 1872—involving the detention of a Peruvian ship in a Japanese port on charges, presented by the British *chargé d'affaires*, that the ship was carrying a cargo of Chinese "slaves"—may have contributed to the lapsing of the convention on immigration. On the incident, see de Arona, Juan, *La Immigración en el Perú*, Lima, 1891, p. 17. In the next year the importation of Chinese into Peru was also stopped.

[14] For the text of the treaty, see Dancuart, P. E., *Anales de la Hacienda Pública del Perú*, Lima, 1908, X (1875-8), pp. 168-70.

were not, as has been claimed, "the first Japanese to come to South America,"[15] since the Peruvian census of 1876 had reported 15 Japanese citizens residing in the country. Nevertheless, they did represent the first real wave of Japanese immigration, and were at least earlier than the much larger flood of migration to Brazil, which began about 1908. Although this was only a minor episode in the great migratory movements which characterized the end of the 19th century, it possessed a peculiar character.

Under the presidency of Piérola, Peru was at that time experiencing a period of rapid growth and consolidation. New social institutions, far-reaching economic reforms, and audacious projects and proposals stimulated the development of the country, whose wounds, more than ten years after the Treaty of Ancon, seemed to have healed. Mining industries were just beginning to show signs of revival. The low price of silver discouraged many enterprises, and copper was not yet being exploited in Cerro de Pasco. The rubber boom had not yet started. Communications with the Sierras were still very poor. It was coastal agriculture, therefore, which received the first stimulus, and it reacted promptly.

[15] Requien, M., *Le problème de la population au Japon*, Tokyo, 1934, p. 115. In a more cautious manner, Levasseur stated that the 50,000 Orientals living in Peru in 1876 were "presque tous Chinois" (*La population française*, Paris, 1892, III p. 461, n. 2). Beals erred in the opposite direction in apparently believing that Japanese and Chinese immigrants came to Peru together, or at least in the same years (e.g., *Fire on the Andes*, pp. 82, 399). I cannot find any confirmation of Hodges' statement that there were over 900 Japanese working for the British sugar company near Cañete at a considerably earlier date than 1899 ("Japanese Ambitions in Latin America," *Sunset* Magazine, October 1916, pp. 16-17).

At once more laborers were needed; this labor had to be cheap, because of the competition from producers of beet sugar. Sugar-cane plantations require armies of peons as permanent labor forces. Whence could they be obtained? All attempts to foster immigration and colonization by Europeans had failed miserably. Foreign governments which looked after their emigrants, like the Italian for example, strongly advised their people against migrating to Peru.[16] Besides, until the opening of the Panama Canal, Peru was much farther from Europe than from Asia.

Peru had already experimented with Asiatics, having introduced almost 100,000 Chinese during the prosperous "guano period" (1849-74). Public opinion, expressed by riots and massacres, was strongly opposed to these cheap competitors in agricultural labor and the smaller trades. Nothing, however, had been done with Japanese, though Japan is geographically the nearest to Peru of any part of Asia. The Chinese were commonly referred to in Peru as "Asiatics," and consequently the term "Asiatic" had acquired a distinctly derogatory meaning, which included all natives of Asia. However, the Sino-Japanese war in 1895 had demonstrated that Asia was composed of different peoples. Peru determined to discover whether the Japanese would be useful immigrants.

Japan, on its part, was undergoing an expansionist period and was becoming preoccupied with emigration problems. The Japanese Act for the Protection of

[16] Italians came, however, but almost none as *brazos*. They came as skilled workers, traders, representatives, etc.

Emigrants was passed in 1896. In 1898 Japanese migration to Hawaii—there were 30,000 Japanese settlers there by 1894—and the Philippines suffered a decisive setback with American occupation of these islands. Other outlets had to be sought. The organization of emigration to Peru was more of an experiment than anything else. Like almost all earlier attempts at immigration to Peru, it was an official affair. With the full support of the Peruvian Government, two undertakings were initiated in 1897, one by the Peruvian Consul in Yokohama, the other and more important one by Morioka and Company in Tokyo.

The conditions of the agreement were severe but relatively humane. Prospective immigrants had to be between 20 and 45 years of age, and had to be willing to work ten hours daily in the fields or twelve hours in mills or workshops. The landowners were to pay them ten pounds for travel expenses and two pounds and a half monthly, in addition to providing lodgings and medical care. The wives were to receive only one and a half pounds, and no travel allowance (so that practically no women came to Peru). At the expiration of the contract, the return journey was to be paid for by the immigration agency, whose representative in Peru was the only authorized intermediary between landowner and colonist.[17] It is clear that what was envisaged was nothing more than a temporary immi-

[17] Sacchetti, Alfredo, *Immigrantes para el Perú*, Turin, 1904, p. 11; del Rio, Mario E., *La Inmigración y su desarrollo en el Perú*, Lima, 1929, pp. 61-2. See also the comments of the British observer Martin on the Japanese working on the sugar estates and rubber forests (Martin, *Peru of the Twentieth Century*, London, 1911, p. 125).

gration of people who would eventually return to Japan. The necessity of working off the cost of the long voyage from Japan to Peru made the immigrants sign on for several years of labor.

About 1,200 Japanese came to Peru, most of them during 1898, but by the end of the century a third of them had already returned to Japan.[18] Those who remained were not highly regarded. They were accused of disorderly and turbulent conduct, of provoking strife with *Cholos* and Chinese, of bringing and spreading new diseases. In the end practically all of them abandoned agriculture and became domestic servants, small shopkeepers, proprietors of little coffeehouses, vendors of ice-cream and soft drinks, makers of sweetmeats, etc., just as the Chinese had done before them.

Another attempt to bring in more Japanese was made in 1903 and at the beginning of 1904, but with even less success. Of the 984 cultivators who arrived with this second wave, almost half died in the sugarcane fields around Cañete, and in the north.[19] Some Japanese continued to arrive in small isolated groups, practically always at the request of Peruvian landowners, with no intention of settling down and with-

[18] The same source which gives this figure of 1,200 arrivals (Requien, *loc. cit.*) says that in 1899 there were 790 Japanese in Peru. Ikeyama, K., who seems to be better informed, says that the first 800 Japanese arrived in 1899, under four-year contracts to some important sugar haciendas—Caudivilla, Huayto, Cayaltí, San Nicolás, La Estrella, Puente Piedra, Casa Blanca, etc. (*La Prensa*, Sept. 30, 1937).

[19] Ikeyama, *loc. cit.* As causes of this high mortality rate, he indicates epidemics, excessive labor, etc. This historical account was accepted by Salinas Cossio, who wrote: "Responde en buena parte a la verdad de los acontecimientos," and discussed only two minor points.

out causing serious alarm. There was no objection to their engaging in agricultural labor, and only a slow-growing reluctance to allow them to become established in towns or certain industries. They were still considered as useful labor, but already as undesirable "people."

Peruvian suspicions of the Japanese grew during and after the Russo-Japanese war, which revealed Japan as an imperialist nation. At the same time, however, there was an increase in Japanese prestige and in the Peruvian reluctance to give offense to Japan.[20] When asked by the Senate for its opinion of a bill forbidding mass Asiatic immigration, the *Sociedád Nacional Agraria,* the organ of the landowners, appointed a commission whose report (published in *Agricultor Peruano,* September 16, 1905) was generally favorable to permitting immigration if it could be controlled. More noteworthy was the report of the Chief of the Immigration Section of the Ministry of Agriculture. Referring to the Chinese, he observed that the golden age of Peruvian agriculture had coincided with their immigration as laborers, and denied that there need be any danger of international complications as long as the immigrants were treated humanely. He added, significantly, that the real danger was rather that the imposition of prohibitions against

[20] An editorial in *La Prensa,* Sept. 2, 1937, declared that Japanese victories over Russia "deluded" Peruvians, who thought that they had found in the Japanese cultivator "el apropiado bracero," only to discover, with sad surprise, that Japanese soon deserted the fields, founded small industries and opened shops in towns. If and when they returned to the earth, it was no longer as humble peons, but "to command as *yanacones,* as great leaseholders, and even as proprietors."

immigration might offend "the excessive pride and suspicion" of the countries against which the prohibitions were directed. Summarizing these tendencies, Garland (*Reseña Industrial del Perú*) suggested that immigration could be limited to workers between 20 and 40 years of age, in good health and under a labor contract not longer than six years, after which time the agency which had brought them to Peru would be bound to repatriate them. They could also be forbidden to reside in towns or to enter certain industries.[21]

A third wave of 774 immigrants arrived in Peru in 1906 under contract to work on the haciendas of Paramonga, Laredo, Chacra Cerro, San Nicolás, Huachipa and others in the Cañete Valley. In 1907, in view both of the high mortality rate among Japanese colonists in Peru, and the growing objections to Japanese immigration on the North American Pacific coast, the Japanese Government decided to permit emigration only to countries where Japanese settlers would be welcome. In 1908, 800 Japanese went to Brazil, where they established a promising colony on land granted to them by the Government.

A few years later Garcia Calderon wrote: "La terre, qui manque de serfs chinois, est ainsi fécondée par des immigrants japonais." (*Les Démocraties Latines de l'Amérique*, Paris, 1914, p. 306). Calderon gave the first account of the "Japanese menace" and saw the danger as mainly political. He opposed the thesis of the Argentine writer Manuel Ugarte that antagonism between

---

[21] See Pesce, L., *Indigenas e Inmigrantes*, Lima, 1906, pp. 118-24.

THE PAST 73

Japan and the United States could be usefully exploited by Latin American countries.

In Peru during these years the rubber boom rose and then collapsed (1911-12). It evoked a great many schemes and projects of immigration and colonization. But there was almost no concern with a specific Japanese problem; no distinction was made between Chinese and Japanese in Peru. Asiatics as such were undesirable. According to Peruvian statistics, there were in Peru only 621 Japanese in 1908, or three per cent of the total number of resident foreigners. Four years later, Lord Bryce summarized the situation thus: "In Peru . . . the Chinese and Japanese who come are too few to affect the character of the population . . . Any danger of this nature seems remote and improbable."[22]

But the migration continued. According to a Japanese-Peruvian source, by 1922 no less than 83 groups of Japanese, totaling some 20,000, had arrived in Peru. The same source states that only 20 per cent of this number remained and sent to Japan for their families to join them.[23] As a result of internal migration, which increased during the first World War, most of these

[22] Bryce, J., *South America: Observations and Impressions*, New York, 1932, pp. 438, 504. It is noteworthy that even such a shrewd observer as Bryce failed to distinguish between Chinese and Japanese. See also the quotations from *El Comercio* (1904, 1905, 1907, 1908, *et seq.*) in *El Comercio, Numero del Centenario*, May 4, 1939, p. 26. The Chinese "danger" was removed by the Porras-Wu Ting-fang Agreement (August 28, 1909), which put an end to Chinese immigration to Peru. All later attacks against "Oriental" or "Asiatic" immigrants, and all related restrictive measures, were, therefore, specifically anti-Japanese.

[23] Ikeyama, *loc. cit.* In 1923 immigration under contract was suppressed (Toru Ogishima, quoted by Salinas Cossio in *La Prensa*, Oct. 19, 1937).

survivors left the farm lands and wandered to towns and cities in search of a more independent existence.

From 1914 to 1939

The next wave of immigration came during and after the first World War. For the first time Japanese exports to Peru rose to figures of some importance, and the merger in 1917 of 54 private agencies in the officially sponsored Kaigai Kogyo Kaisha (Overseas Development Corporation) provided an instrument for

ARRIVALS AND DEPARTURES OF JAPANESE CITIZENS
(Peruvian statistics)

	Arrivals	Departures	Difference
1926	1,362	416	946
1927*	1,036	256	780
1928†	1,359	643	716
1934	640	976	−336
1935	608	1,111	−503
1936	681	801	−120
1937	294	940	−646
1938	292	692	−400
1939	243	658	−415

* According to statistics, of the "passengers" arriving, instead of "foreigners" admitted, the arrivals were 1,595, the departures 531.
† The figures represent "passengers" arriving and leaving.

the promotion and protection of Japanese emigration. With the financial assistance of the Government, which offered passages at reduced fares or even completely free, the K. K. K. brought 2,933 emigrants to Peru before the end of 1930.[24] In that year the Japanese

[24] Requien, *op. cit.*, pp. 119-124. In the same years the K.K.K. carried 14,000 emigrants to the Philippines, 73,000 to Brazil, and many others elsewhere. See also Zischka, *op. cit.*, p. 59; Bradley, *op. cit.* p. 54 ff; Kawada, *Situation de l' Emigration Japonaise*, 1933, pp. 491, 494.

Census showed 20,650 Japanese subjects living in Peru. Peruvian figures were somewhat lower: in 1920 they reported 4,622 Japanese resident in Lima and Callao provinces, and 9,782 were counted there in the 1926 Census. In 1925 Dunn estimated that there were 10,000 Japanese in the entire country. Taking into account the small groups settled in other coast provinces or in the interior (Huánuco, Junín, Madre de Dios), and inasmuch as Peruvian statistics do not consider as "foreigners" Japanese children born in Peru and therefore Peruvians *jure soli*, the Japanese Census figures were probably the more accurate. Japanese had already become the most important foreign colony in Peru, surpassing the old Chinese colony, which had been partially absorbed through intermarriage. Yet it was a gross exaggeration to declare that "Peru is saturated with Japanese workmen and peasants."[25]

Among the main factors contributing to this rapid rise, besides the activity of the K. K. K., there were the growing prosperity of Peru during the Leguia decade, as a result of sound internal economic development and unsound United States loans, and the Federal Immigration Act which closed the United States to Japanese and forced them to seek new outlets if emigration was to continue.[26] Although statistics disagree, and in any case are never easy to interpret, they reveal that the bulk of the new Japanese immigration occurred between 1925 and 1930. According to Japanese figures, 7,269 Japanese migrated to Peru during these years.

[25] *Enciclopedia Italiana*, XVII (1933), p. 19.
[26] In 1929 Japan established a Ministry for Overseas Affairs (Emigration and Colonization).

What sort of people were they? Anything but agricultural laborers. They were small traders, artisans, cultivators, or workers skilled in a few traditional lines (rubber workers, plumbers, watch-makers, opticians, and the like), and for the most part they were relatives or friends of established Japanese residents.

The arrival at Callao of a returning Japanese or of a newcomer was a curious and moving spectacle. A whole row of Peruvian-Japanese acquaintances would greet the new arrival with innumerable bows, at graduated distances, with radiant smiles and friendly questions. The newcomer felt at home immediately, and not lost in an unknown and perhaps hostile land. He would be assisted through the customs, helped by interpreters, and then escorted ceremoniously to town.[27]

The world depression created a new attitude among Peruvians. Hitherto there had been only a dim awareness of a racial danger, and in some areas the pressure of industrial competition. But with the devaluation of the Japanese yen, and the rising proportion of Japa-

[27] Exact data are lacking about the regions of Japan from which these people came. It appears, however, that a large group are from the island of Okinawa, midway between Japan and Formosa. This would be interesting, especially if it was not accidental, because Okinawa has a climate (subtropical, healthy, oceanic and moist) which is much more like the Peruvian than the climate of the main Japanese islands; because only after 1895 was Japan's title to Okinawa no longer disputed, and emigration to Peru started in 1897-98; because the most important crop and article of trade in Okinawa was sugar cane, as was the case in Peru also about 1898 (see "Luchu Archipelago," in *Encyclopaedia Britannica*, 11th edition).

In the second of his articles on "La Inmigración en el Brasil y el Problema Japonés" (*La Prensa*, Sept. 10, 1937), Prof. Henry Hauser stated that at least half of the 150,000 Japanese in Brazil came from central and southern Japan.

THE PAST 77

nese imports in Peru's foreign trade, Peruvians awoke to a third menace, a commercial one. This of course helped to revitalize the old and half-forgotten misgivings. Mistakes in conduct by the Japanese colony, aggressive merchandizing methods, and the new wave of nationalism which characterized the Benavides presidency, contributed to the growth of suspicion and dislike of Japanese. The Japanese-Peruvian Treaty of Commerce, concluded in 1928, was denounced in 1934.[28] In 1935 the influential *Asociación de Comercio e Industrias de Arequipa* published a message to the President of the Republic, asking protection against Japanese and Chinese immigration and commercial infiltration.[29] And finally a new immigration law, aimed against Japanese "invasion," was promulgated on June 26, 1936, and implemented by further strict regulations on May 15, 1937. Ultimately, as a reaction to the increasing number of Japanese farmers, especially in a few cotton-growing valleys near Lima, a fourth danger was discovered. This was the threat offered by alleged Japanese land-grabbing, or the rural Japanese menace. Denounced as early as 1934 by Salinas Cossio, this last danger was the main argument during the fierce campaign waged against Japanese infiltration by *La Prensa* from August to November 1937.

This campaign coincided with the Japanese offen-

[28] The text appears in the *Boletin de la Cámara de Comercio de Lima,* VI (1935), pp. 548-9.
[29] Salinas Cossio stated that his series of articles in 1934 awakened the government to the danger and eventually provoked the denunciation of the Treaty (*La Prensa*, August 21, 1937).

sive in Shanghai and the interior of China. On the front page of the newspaper, big headlines announced attacks, bombings, massacres, and bloody triumphs of Japanese arms. On October 5 the League of Nations pronouncement of Japanese war guilt was featured. On later pages the Japanese menace to Peru was daily denounced and analyzed. Does the Japanese colony constitute a real danger? asked one contributor who replied: "Yes, it does represent a political peril. The rumble of cannon-fire in China gives us proof."[30] Even more outspoken was the correspondent who declared that there were more than 40,000 Japanese in Peru, and hinted at the possibility of their serving as a pretext for armed intervention by their homeland, "as is now happening in Manchuria."[31]

The controversy dragged on for more than three months. The chief adversaries were Salinas Cossio as "prosecutor" and Ikeyama, the able editor of *Peru Jiho*, as "defendant," but a score of other writers took part. Editorials in *La Prensa* supported Salinas Cossio. Practically all of the arguments *pro* and *con* were stated with the customary courtesy and prolixity.

As a matter of fact, the number of Japanese arrivals in Peru in 1937-39 was less than half the number of those in 1934-36. And, according to official figures, the number of those who left the country between May 1, 1933, and December 8, 1939 (the Benavides period),

[30] *La Prensa*, Sept. 18, 1937. The argument began immediately after the Peruvian Government had taken strong measures against Japanese immigration.
[31] *La Prensa*, Sept. 24, 1937. Another contributor emphasized that the Japanese Government was using "todos los medios; las armas en China, las subvenciones en el Perú" (*La Prensa*, August 24, 1937).

was almost double that of those who arrived.[32] It is not unlikely that the new Japanese drive in Manchuria and China attracted prospective Japanese emigrants to these nearer regions. The last outburst of anti-Japanese feeling occurred on May 13, 1940. Inflamed by the false rumor that firearms had been found in Japanese haciendas,[33] and without heeding immediate official denials, some elements of the populace of Lima and Callao attacked and sacked a number of Japanese shops and bazaars. Claims for damages amounting to about two million soles were filed through the Chamber of Commerce and the Japanese Consulate. The Peruvian Govern-

[32] On August 26, 1940, in response to an inquiry by former Foreign Minister Concha, Foreign Minister Solf y Muro gave these figures on Japanese arrivals in and departures from Peru.

Year	Arrivals	Departures
1933 (May 1–Dec. 31)	195	432
1934	640	976
1935	608	1,111
1936	681	801
1937	294	940
1938	292	692
1939 (Jan. 1–Dec. 8)	243	658

He added that the "arrivals" included "temporary visitors," and "departures" included those who left with re-entry permits (*El Comercio*, Sept. 11, 1940). "Arrivals" also included those with re-entry permits.

[33] Perhaps because of some purchases made by the Peruvian Government in 1934-35, "Japanese arms in Peru" have been a recurrent tale, a sort of "ritual crime," denounced and utilized for different ends. De Lauwe (*op. cit.*, p. 208) writes "La communauté japonaise achète des avions." Beals (*op. cit.*, pp. 445-6) states that Peru, "preparing for the Leticia trouble," bought Japanese ammunition for eighty million soles (!), paying for it with guano (!). Whitaker, John T. (*Americas to the South*, New York, 1939) relates that the Japanese colony promised Benavides "that if the regime is threatened they can put 5,000 armed men into the field to aid the dictator" (p. 17), and to "fight for him if he wants to shoot down the Apristas" (p. 31). The same author states that Japanese "have bought all the water frontage in the town of Chimbote, a perfect

ment accepted responsibility in principle,[34] an official commission was appointed to determine the losses,[35] and on September 23, 1941, the Minister of Finance asked Parliament for an extraordinary appropriation of 1,424,506 soles to indemnify the Japanese citizens and "some Peruvian nationals" for damages suffered.[36] Toward the end of the year, propaganda leaflets were again circulated, accusing the Japanese of espionage, of possessing concealed firearms, and so on. Against such accusations the editor of the Japanese paper *Peru Jiho* wrote a letter which contained perhaps exaggerated expressions of loyalty,[37] thus provoking a fierce reac-

---

deep-sea anchorage or naval base" (p. 35). A similar hint was dropped by Salinas Cossio (*La Prensa*, Sept. 21, 1937), who said that many "modest" and "poor-looking" Japanese are in reality intellectuals, professional men and "hasta jefes del ejército y de la marina de su país." It is known, too, that during the last border incidents the Ecuadoreans declared that Japanese troops were fighting with the Peruvian forces. Such rumors had already been common in Ecuador for months before the incident, and were denied by a Peruvian general (see note 2, p. 2).

[34] In some quarters, the earthquake of May 24, which caused considerable damage to Lima, Callao and environs, was thought to be the speedy answer of the Japanese gods, even more vindictive than Japanese statesmen.

[35] *Boletín de la Cámara de Comercio de Lima*, XI (1940), p. 227.

[36] *El Comercio*, Sept. 24, 1941. The Chamber of Deputies approved this appropriation on October 29, 1941 (*El Comercio,* Oct. 30, 1941), and was followed by the Senate on November 11, 1941 (*ibid.*, Nov. 12, 1941). It was stated that the Japanese were going to receive 1,400,000 soles, and the Peruvians 24,506. The Japanese actually received only 350,000 soles in money; the rest was paid in Peruvian produce, 600,000 soles in wool, 250,000 in salt and 200,000 in sugar. (*Revista de Hacienda*, no. 7, 1941, pp. 392-3.)

[37] "A los japoneses aquí residentes no les anima el propósito de volver a su patria de origen. Aquí trabajan, aquí tienen su hogar y aquí piensan morir . . . aman al Perú como a su segunda patria . . . ya nada los une a su país de origen, al que ni piensan retornar . . . cualquiera que sea el giro que tomen los asuntos internacionales, nuestra actitud será la misma, ya que nada tenemos que hacer con lo que ocurre en otros pueblos,

tion, especially in Huancayo.[38] Happily the dispute remained in the journalistic stage. During 1941, there was a distinct improvement in relations with the Japanese community, partly owing to the development of closer business contacts and partly as a reaction against Ecuadorean accusations that Japanese troops were fighting with Peruvians against Ecuador.

---

siendo nuestro deseo permanecer aquí y rendir al Perú el fruto de nuestro trabajo . . . el japonés inculca a sus hijos a venerar y servir con fidelidad el suelo que los vió nacer, su patria única y verdadera: el Perú (letter in *El Universal,* Dec. 6, 1940). The letter also invited any Peruvian to attend any meeting of the Japanese colony.

[38] See *La Crónica,* Jan. 11, 1941, quoting *Comercio e Industria* of Huancayo. The latter paper interpreted the Japanese attachment to the new fatherland as follows: "Here we came, and we decided to remain, and we shall not go away because we wish to remain . . ."

II. THE PRESENT

Demographic Aspects

Unreliable though statistics may be, it is possible by dint of comparison and checking with other data to estimate the number of Japanese citizens and Japanese-born Peruvian citizens residing in Peru at between 20,000 and 25,000. The main difficulties in determining the size of the Japanese colony are the absence (until June 1940) of a thorough census,[1] the *jus soli* regulation according to which Japanese children born in Peru are considered as Peruvians, and the marked mobility of the colony. Many children and young people are sent to Japan to study. Numerous old people return to die in the motherland. Traveling agents and commercial travelers are numerous. On the other hand, the geographical concentration of the bulk of the colony in a few areas is helpful to the investigator.

At any rate, even Guevara, the last writer to denounce the Japanese "peril," speaks of only 30,000 Japanese in Peru.[2] And even in the heat of the *La*

[1] A census has now been taken, but only provisional results have been published. "Asiatics," comprising Chinese and Japanese (classified according to racial origin and not by country of birth), were reported to number 41,945.
[2] *Op. cit.*, p. 137.

THE PRESENT 83

Prensa debate no higher figure than 40,000 was advanced with evidence of any kind.[3] Indeed, there is some reason to believe that the Japanese do not number even 25,000.

Members of the Japanese colony mostly intermarry among themselves. Whereas Chinese, like the first Spaniards, came to Peru without wives and mingled freely with all sorts of natives—with Cholos and Negroes and mestizos—thus originating some of the most interesting racial cross-breeds in Peru, the Japanese (when they no longer came under contract) have shown a marked tendency to arrive with their wives, or even in family groups.[4] When a young bachelor wishes to marry, he often sends to Japan for a wife.[5] Otherwise he marries a Peruvian-born Japanese girl. This practice is in striking contrast to that of other foreign groups in Peru. In 1939 all other foreign (non-Japanese) nationalities registered more births from mixed (Peruvian-foreign) marriages than from marriages between members of the same foreign nationality.

Japanese provided the only exception, and a marked one it was. A total of 766 births were recorded by Japanese parents, as against 146 by a Japanese father and a Peruvian mother, three by a Japanese father and a Bolivian mother, and one by a Japanese father and a

[3] In a letter in *La Prensa*, Sept. 24, 1937: "Hay más de 40,000 japoneses en el país." The figure was denied, as being grossly exaggerated, by the Japanese Akio Banno (*ibid.*, Oct. 4, 1937).

[4] During the few years (1924-27) for which there are detailed figures, the proportion of women to men immigrating to Peru was higher for the Japanese than for any other important national group.

[5] Dunn, ordinarily very well informed, commits the error of saying that "Japanese intermarry freely with the lower classes of natives" (*Peru*, Washington, 1925, p. 23).

Turkish mother. The contrast becomes still more striking if it is considered that a number of "Peruvian" mothers were probably Peruvian-born Japanese girls. On the other side of the picture, only 79 Chinese children were born of Chinese parents, as against 268 born of a Chinese father and a Peruvian mother.

In 1939 there were only 18 "Japanese" marriages, or one per mille of the total number (18,000) of marriages celebrated in Peru; and of these only four marriages were of Japanese with Japanese, as against 14 of Japanese with Peruvians. In 1940, 25 Japanese men were married, 19 to Peruvian women and 6 to Japanese women. It is likely that not all Japanese marriages celebrated in Peru are registered before the Peruvian authorities, and that most of the relatively few marriages in which the wife is a Peruvian are celebrated according to Peruvian law. It is also probable that a number of "Peruvian" girls are really Peruvian-born Japanese. At any rate, the figure of one per mille appears to be misleading—especially in view of the abnormally high birth rate (almost five per cent) which statistics attribute to the Japanese colony, in comparison with that of the Chinese and every other national group.[6]

[6] Dr. C. E. Paz Soldan became alarmed when the birth rate averaged 4% (*La Prensa*, Oct. 3, 1937). What he feared for Peru was crudely expressed as "la niponización del vientre." As a matter of fact, the number of marriages between Japanese (in 1939 only four were registered) bears no relation to the number of children born of two Japanese parents (766). The larger number of children registered as "Peruvians" and not, as formerly, at the Japanese Consulate, caused alarm (*ibid.*, Oct. 21, 1937). The situation was similar in 1940 when 748 children were born of Japanese mothers, 740 of them having Japanese fathers. There were 175 children having Japanese fathers and "Peruvian" mothers.

Where do the Japanese settle? The great majority, more than eighty per cent of the total, live in the Department of Lima and in Callao Province, comprising not only the capital and the most important port of the country, but also some of the richest cotton-growing valleys. Other sizable groups are to be found in Junin, the greatest mineral district (comprising Cerro de Pasco, La Oroya and Huancayo,[7] and in the rice- and sugar-producing north coastal departments of La Libertad and Lambayaque. These departments, connected with each other by excellent asphalt roads, are the richest and most progressive part of the country. Some smaller groups of Japanese live in other comparatively prosperous coastal departments (Ancash, Ica). The Sierra and Montaña regions have only a few scattered families. From some areas, among them the great Puno Department in the south, they are completely absent. Their geographical concentration draws more public attention to them.

Economic Aspects

Agriculture. How much land have the Japanese bought up? What proportion of agricultural production are they responsible for? Unfortunately, on these questions there are more controversial statements than reliable statistics. Passions run high because of the sentimental value attached to landownership, and also because cultivable land is very scarce on the Peruvian

[7] On the Huancayo group, established about 1920 by a hairdresser, "que resultó ser un experto organizador y financista" (the very reincarnation of Figaro!), see the impassioned letter in *La Prensa,* Oct. 16, 1937, denouncing the "odioso monopolio" of Japanese tradesmen.

coast.[8] Salinas Cossio estimated in 1934 that 15 per cent of the coastal cotton crop was produced by Japanese; and in 1937 he raised this estimate to between 20 and 25 per cent.[9] He acknowledged that the percentage of Japanese production was higher than the percentage of land area cultivated by Japanese, because, he explained, the Japanese had chosen the "most fertile and least risky" valleys, and also, it is safe to add, because the Japanese obtains greater production than the native from the same area.

Moreover, the percentage of land area cultivated by Japanese is, in its turn, much larger than the percentage of land area owned by them, since the largest part of the cultivated area is held by the Japanese as *yanacones*. Yanacones are share-croppers who pay the landowners an annual fixed quantity of cotton, normally (around Lima) between 30 and 40 Spanish quintals (46 kilograms) of unginned cotton per *fane-*

[8] There is no contradiction in the scarcity of land and the scarcity of labor. Rather there is a link between these two phenomena: the combination of the very high price of land and of very low wages is unattractive to laborers, who cannot hope to become landed proprietors. For a discussion of this state of affairs, see Ferrero, R. A., *Tierra y Población en el Perú: La Escasez de Tierras Cultivadas y sus Consecuencias*, Lima, 1938.

[9] Salinas Cossio, "La Infiltración Japonesa, I: La Colonia Japonesa y la Producción Agrícola," *La Prensa*, August 21, 1937. This article began the long debate already referred to. In another article (*ibid.*, Sept. 21, 1937), answering the accusation of "gross exaggeration" (by Ikeyama, *ibid.*, Sept. 7, 1937), Salinas Cossio explained that he had calculated this percentage of 20 to 25 per cent from three statistical bases: (1) the list of properties visibly exploited by Japanese (which he did not publish because he wished to avoid "personalities"); (2) their consumption of guano; and (3) the water taxes which they paid. Obviously (2) and (3) stand or fall with (1). On Sept. 14, 1937, he repeated that the land-buying program was in his estimation the most dangerous aspect of the Japanese "infiltration," or, more than a danger, a "real and present nuisance."

gada (three hectares). This is equivalent to about 400-500 pounds per acre. Most of the share-croppers rent small or medium-size farms (from 10 to 25 hectares) for a number of years, ordinarily paying, in addition to the annual payment of cotton, a *juanillo* or *prime*, when they first obtain the farm. The juanillo of course varies with the value of the farm. Where the ground has still to be broken for cultivation, there may be no juanillo or, in some cases, the cultivator may pay less cotton for the first year than for the following ones.

Through this system, which goes back to Inca times (when the yanacon was more like a serf attached to the land), the Japanese have penetrated extensively in the Chancay Valley, immediately north of Lima, and to a lesser extent in the Chillón and Rimac (Lima) Valleys. In consequence, Peruvian landowners have commonly been accused of forgetting their patriotic duties in return for "1,000 soles juanillos per fanegada on long-term leases."[10] In 12 big haciendas in the Chancay (Huaral) Valley, with 827 yanacones, 50 per cent are Japanese.[11]

[10] Cossio, Salinas, *La Prensa*, August 21, 1937; Badani, J., President of the *Asociación Rural del Perú, ibid.*, Oct. 30, 1937. A *Sociedad Nacional Agraria* inquiry in 1935 revealed that in Rimac (Lima) Valley, Japanese yanacones paid annual cotton fees amounting to as much as from 32 to 35 quintals in addition to a juanillo of from 2,500 to 3,000 soles (*Como se produce el algodón en el Perú*, Lima, 1936, p. 250). In Surco Valley (near Lima) the annual payment amounted to 35 quintals, plus a juanillo of 500 soles and other expenses—"condiciones que no pueden ser igualadas por los nacionales" (*ibid.*, p. 50). Even a state-owned farm, also in Surco Valley, was exploited mainly by Japanese yanacones (*ibid., pp.* 46-7). A. Ulloa, who, as a Minister, signed the law against Japanese yanacones, has nothing but praise for their excellent qualities as cultivators (*Posición Internacional del Perú*, Lima, 1941, pp. 349-50).

[11] Ñañes, Victor, "Régimen de explotación de los fundos algodoneros," *Boletín de la Compañia Administradora del Guano*, XVII (1941), pp.

In the Chancay Valley there are also important Japanese properties, one of which (owned by N. Okada and Company) is said to exploit almost 40 per cent of the total area under cotton in the valley. In the urban centers of the same valley (Chancay, Huaral), most of the laboratories, shops, and the like are operated by Japanese,[12] who in most cases have displaced Chinese rather than Peruvians. However, Chancay Valley, comprising some seven per cent of the total area under cotton, but taking about ten per cent of the guano utilized in cotton cultivation, produces no more than from 8.5 per cent (1937) to ten per cent (1940) of the total Peruvian cotton crop. Even if the Chancay Valley crop were produced entirely by Japanese (and the

---

251-3. Other figures, which look less reliable, were given by X. Y. Z. in *La Prensa*, August 27, 1937, and by Gonzales, Pedro, "La Ocupacion Japonesa de los Valles de Huaral y Chancay," *ibid.*, Sept. 4, 1937. The latter affirmed that 90% of the Huaral Valley area was in Japanese hands, that in Chancay 2,407 fanegadas were being exploited by Japanese, and that the big Japanese proprietors had helped smaller Japanese cultivators and shopkeepers to overcome Chinese competition. The same figure of 2,407 fanegadas (7,200 hectares) is given by J. M. R. y G. (*ibid.*, Sept. 26, 1937), according to whom there are, besides, three haciendas with 1,900 hectares cultivated by Chinese. Almost 3,000 hectares (out of a total of 72,000 in Chancay Valley) belong to five Peruvian haciendas, but four of them employ a high percentage of Japanese cultivators.

[12] But it is an exaggeration to say that such centers look completely Japanese, or that "quien visite Huaral en día de fiesta, no puede dejar de sentirse en país extraño donde flamean las banderas japonesas con profusión y continuidad" (Guevara, *op. cit.*, pp. 137, 146-7, citing Gonzales, Pedro M., *op. cit.*). The author was in Huaral on a Sunday. Not a Japanese flag was in sight; not even Japanese inscriptions were to be seen; and the people, though many of them were evidently of Japanese origin, were not to be distinguished, by their dress or occupation, from true Peruvians. Also, the buildings in Huaral and Chancay look like those in any other Peruvian town.

most extreme estimates do not exceed 90 per cent)[13] and even if the less conspicuous Japanese production in the other valleys were added,[14] experts agree that the total would hardly exceed 15 per cent of the total Peruvian cotton crop.

The concentration of Japanese agriculture in a single valley is easy to explain. Chancay Valley is the first fertile valley north of Lima. Most of the Japanese who did not migrate there from Lima were secured from Japan under contract by an important Peruvian *hacendado* who treated them so well that they remained after the expiration of their contracts.[15] Then through mutual assistance and possibly with the help of loans granted by their central organization, they grew in number, in accord with the typical tendency of Japanese colonies to proliferate while remaining in compact localized groups.

Their specialization in cotton has been a result of economic factors. Cotton is the safest and most important crop on the Peruvian coast. It is not difficult to grow, but it requires much care, and the Japanese have proved adept at raising it. There seems to be little reason to suspect the existence of a plan organized "by farsighted Japanese statesmen" (Salinas Cossio) for the

[13] Gonzales, *op. cit.* The *Sociedad Nacional Agraria* estimated (1935) that the Japanese yanacones (in the Japanese-administered haciendas) amount to 80%, and the Peruvian ones to 20% (*Como se produce el algodón, op. cit.,* p. 40).

[14] On some large haciendas in Rimac (Lima) Valley in 1935 up to 90% of the yanacones were Japanese (*ibid.,* p. 250). Japanese lessees were also in Comas Valley (see *ibid.,* p. 234), and yanacones were on the increase in other minor valleys around Lima.

[15] Ikeyama, K., "Nuevos puntos sobre nuevas ies," *La Prensa,* Sept. 25, 1937.

monopoly of cotton cultivation, notwithstanding that also in Brazil and Mexico Japanese cultivators have concentrated on this crop.[16] The entire Peruvian crop is comparatively unimportant in world production. The Japanese growers normally sell their cotton to Peruvian middlemen or to American and English agents. Only in 1935-36, and to an even greater degree in 1939-1941, did Japan buy a substantial percentage of Peruvian cotton exports, partly because of the dislocation of its normal markets.

The only other Japanese agricultural activities worth mentioning are in the most accessible zones of the Amazon forest, where two or three concessions have been granted to Japanese. The first, a thousand hectares in the Chanchamayo Valley, was obtained by the *Peru Takushoku Kumiai* in 1931 from the Peruvian Corporation [17] for the production of maize, coffee and other crops. The company is a cooperative, financed entirely by Japanese residents, and it is emerging slowly from the experimental stage. In 1937 there

[16] Suspicions were voiced by Salinas Cossio, "La Infiltracion Japonesa," *La Prensa*, August 21 and Sept. 21, 1937, after Zischka, *op. cit.*, pp. 59, 286-7, who saw a Japanese plan to become independent of American cotton. The same writer gives a more plausible reason for emigration to Mexico. It was made free, he writes (*op. cit.*, p. 158), in the year of the passage of the United States Federal Immigration Act (1924). The charges were denied by Ikeyama (*La Prensa*, Sept. 29, 1937), and repeated by Behrendt, R. F. ("Foreign Influences in Latin America," *The Annals*, Vol. 204 (1939), p. 3): "Large and continually increasing colonies of Japanese have been sent to these [cotton-growing] countries [including Peru] in order to foster the cultivation of cotton."

[17] The Peruvian Corporation is a British-controlled company which operates the most important Peruvian railways and still owns large subtropical areas obtained in part payment of ancient guano loans.

were (in Perené) only 20 Japanese families, comprising 74 persons.[18]

In the Huallaga region one or two Japanese firms obtained vast concessions which evoked spirited controversies and protests.[19] The drug-importing firm of Nonomiya has started to plant cinchona trees on an area of a thousand hectares, about 40 miles beyond Tingo Maria. It will be necessary to wait eight years before the bark can be utilized. A factory for the production of quinine salts will eventually be installed on the plantation.

The other Japanese concession comprises a reduced and impoverished colony which still lives in Madre de Dios, where Japanese settled during the rubber boom and stayed on when it collapsed.

Commerce and industry. By far the largest number of Japanese in Peru are engaged in retail trade and small industries.[20] That typical institution, the

[18] Ikeyama, K., "Desde el Comercio Minorista hasta las Empresas Colonizadoras de la Montaña," *La Prensa*, Oct. 29, 1937. He adds that the company does not and never will pay a dividend.

[19] Another writer pushed exaggeration to the point of declaring that the concession extended over two million hectares, and of writing: "la montaña está llena de Japoneses" (*La Prensa*, Oct. 1, 1937). See also *ibid.*, Oct. 20 and 21, 1937. Very probably Close was referring to this same concession when he wrote that Hoshi (Hamine) owns in Peru no less than "la plus grande exploitation d'écorce de quinine du monde" (*Le péril japonais, op. cit.*, p. 302). Between 1928 and 1940 Peru exported 890 tons of cinchona, or an average of 68 tons a year. The fact is that in Peru the cinchona tree is nowhere grown on a large scale; in the Japanese colony in Perené, however, experiments have been carried out with seeds imported from Java (Pretel Vidal, A. R., "El problema de las Cinchonas en el Perú," *Boletín de la Dirección de Agricultura, Ganadería y Colonización*, Lima, 1937, No. 26-7, pp. 19, 43, and esp. 101).

[20] Wholesale dealers, including in their number large firms which import drugs, textiles, hardware, etc., depend mainly on the trade of bazaars and small Japanese retailers. In the all-important mining industry, Japanese interests are negligible.

"bazaar," and such trades as tire-repairing were introduced to Peru by Japanese, and are still to a large extent monopolized by them. In other instances Japanese have taken the place of Chinese, and more occasionally of Italians. Only in exceptional cases have they driven important numbers of Peruvians out of business. But in some fields they have been so successful that competing Peruvian firms have undeniably suffered.

Of the first importance in this regard are the bazaars, which are practically monopolized by the Japanese, as a stroll through the shopping districts of Lima makes plain. The four or five departments (out of the 22 in the Republic) which have the most bazaars also have the largest Japanese populations. The commercial success of the bazaars is due to several factors, but probably more to general sales techniques (fixed prices, large turnovers, informal treatment of customers, intensive advertising campaigns, frequent "liquidation" and "inventory" sales, and the featuring of especially cheap articles as "bait,"[21] than to specifically Japanese advantages (direct access to Japanese producers of low-cost goods, strong internal organization, and mutual assistance through such typical means of financing as the *tanomoshi-ko*.[22] Another factor is the Japanese talent for displaying goods and for catering to the market,

[21] A contributor to *La Prensa*, August 31, 1937, disapproved of this last practice on the ground that it diminishes the opportunities of other shopkeepers to sell high-quality goods.
[22] This is a complicated organization which in general uses the fixed contributions, in money or in kind, made by the members for their own financial assistance, in varying amounts for each. For our immediate purposes, the main feature of the *tanomoshi-ko* is its reliance on mutual assistance and trust.

which is so markedly absent in the average *mestizo* or Indian shopkeeper. Japanese businessmen have been most successful in American countries with the largest Indian populations and a "low per capita purchasing power,"[23] where ambitious, high-salaried American and European commercial representatives make little headway. The Japanese trader's patience goes to any lengths to overcome the distrust of the Indian. His low production costs allow him to reduce his prices until his goods are accessible to even the extremely low purchasing power of the poorest Peruvians.[24] But there is no real sympathy between buyers and sellers. The poor Peruvian may find the bazaar useful, and may need it, just as sometimes he needs the pawnshop managed by his Italian or Spanish neighbor, but he dislikes it profoundly, and in some instances he hates it. He feels instinctively that the Japanese earns his living from the toil of the poor, and no one is ever pleased with the knowledge that he is being exploited. He is dimly aware that selling cheap wares, which are inferior to good ones, is an indirect form of usury.[25] And when he can, he takes his revenge, as blindly and furiously as he did in 1940.

Examination of some dozen or more bazaar firms

[23] Beals, *op. cit.*, pp. 442-3, and de Lauwe: "Si le Jaune apparaît à l'Amérique latine comme un intrus, à l'Indien, il lui apparaît comme un frère" (*op. cit.*, p. 208); and, with some exaggeration: "Par sa race, par sa religion, par ses tendances et par ses habitudes, l'Amérique ibérique indienne est tournée vers l'Asia" (*ibid*, p. 210).

[24] Beals, *loc. cit.*, pp. 442-3.

[25] Economists might profitably analyze this form of "real" as opposed to "monetary" usury. This would be a good approach to the problems presented by such ineradicable and "un-economic" economic institutions as the usurer and the peddler.

reveals some common features which go far to explain why it is impossible to give reliable comprehensive figures on their importance or turnover. Almost all are incorporated as "collective" societies, but actually some of the partners assume unlimited responsibility while others risk only their stake in the undertaking. Almost all of them, therefore, operate with a far larger capital than is apparent. The "real" capital may be anything between three and eight or ten times the declared one, which is usually between 50,000 and 200,000 soles. The firms often refuse to disclose figures on their capital, turnover or profits because they fear both Peruvian taxes and Japanese-imposed contributions for the different societies and cooperative bodies of the colony. But the stock in trade is often limited, and margins are extremely narrow.

Most of the societies are transformations of family businesses; and a single family, having subscribed for almost all of the shares, retains full control. In many cases, small blocks of shares are owned by (or allocated to) Japanese employees and clerks who are thus considered as proprietors and are not affected by the law limiting the foreign personnel of any firm to 20 per cent of the total. It is noteworthy that a relatively high number of old Japanese family firms were transformed into share companies just during the years immediately after the passage of that law. On the other hand, it should be noted that the intimate relationship beween proprietors and employees is in perfect accord with the patriarchal structure of many old

SALUDAMOS CON TODO RESPETO AL PATRIOTA Y CULTO PUEBLO PERUANO EN LA FECHA DE SU GLORIOSO ANIVERSARIO NACIONAL.

1821 — 28 DE JULIO — 1941

COLONIA JAPONESA DE JAUJA
COLONIA JAPONESA DE HUANCAYO
COLONIA JAPONESA DE LA OROYA

OFRECEMOS NUESTRO RESPETUOSO SALUDO AL CULTO Y PATRIOTA PUEBLO PERUANO EN LA FECHA DE SU GLORIOSO ANIVERSARIO NACIONAL:

28 DE JULIO DE 1941

Colonia Japonesa de Piura.
Colonia Japonesa de Chiclayo.
Colonia Japonesa de Chimbote.
Coloniaa Japonesa de Huacho.
Colonia Japonesa de Cañete.
Colonia Japonesa de Barranca y San Nicolas.
Colonia Japonesa de Paramonga.
Colonia Japonesa de Huaral y Chancay.
Escuela Inca Gaunen de Huaral.
Colonia Japonesa de Mala.

T. YABUKI
ESQUINA JUNIN Y BOLIVAR.
CASILLA No. 316
TRUJILLO,
PERU.

ROBERTO NAGASAKI
FERREÑAFE - PERU
SALUDA AL PUEBLO PERUANO EN SU ANIVERSARIO PATRIO.

U. MAOKI Y CIA.
CHICLAYO - TUMAN
PANADERIA ♦ VULCANIZACION
♦ BAZAR ♦

CARLOS YANAGUI
MOTUPE — PROVINCIA LAMBAYEQUE
COMERCIANTES POR MENOR
SALUDO AL PUEBLO PERUANO EN SU ANIVERSARIO PATRIO.

DOMINGO SAKATA
— MALA —
ALMACEN DE ABARROTES Y GRAN BAZAR. —— VENTAS POR MAYOR Y MENOR.

JULIO TAO
— CHICLAYO —
SALUDA A SUS AMIGOS PERUANOS Y LES DESEA UN SALUDO DE FIESTAS PATRIAS.
28 de Julio de 1941.

Page from Special Edition of *La Prensa*
July 28, 1941

Japanese firms.[26] In several instances owners and clerks live together in the backrooms of the shop, or at least in the same building.[27]

One characteristic of the bazaars is their dependence, to a considerable extent, on self-financing, mainly through the deposits of relatives. Another is the closeness of their relationship with exporting concerns in Japan. Several Japanese wholesale merchants in Peru export local products such as raw cotton while importing Japanese textiles. They act as agents of firms in Kobe, Yokohama, and Osaka. Some of the biggest bazaars maintain one partner in Japan as their purchasing agent. In a few cases the head office is in Japan, whence it sells goods to different countries through the normal trade channels, and to Peru through its bazaar there which is managed by a son or another relative of the senior partner. Generally, however, the "Peruvian" firm is independent and sells mostly, but not exclusively, Japanese articles that have been bought through a few large wholesale importing concerns which, though much less conspicuous than the bazaars, are reputed to make even larger profits. The bigger dealers often do business in the provinces also. They have only one retail outlet in each town, to avoid competition.

The articles most commonly sold are cheap textiles

[26] Crocker indicates as a manifestation of Japanese patriotism the custom of "employers or other economic superiors realizing and carrying out responsibilities to their dependents in a way unknown to the West" (*The Japanese Population Problem: The Coming Crisis*, London, 1931, p. 221. See also pp. 41-2).

[27] This recalls the "dormitories" of Japanese industrial plants and other instances of a "common life" among employers and employees (see, e.g., Zischka, *op. cit.*, pp. 74-6, 173).

(cotton and silk) and then toilet goods and perfumes, with an admixture of other novelty and sporting goods, toys, household fixtures, etc. Figures on sales are very difficult to obtain, and still more difficult to verify; yet it appears that the turnover amounts to about four times the actual capital invested. About three-quarters of the sales are of Japanese-made articles. Assuming that almost all Japanese imports are sold through these shops, it is possible, though risky, to estimate the probable total commercial capital at between eight and ten million soles,[28] and gross sales at around 25 million soles, or even 30 million in recent years.

These sums, and the profits which they imply, suggest another aspect of Japanese business activities in Peru. This is their inconspicuousness. There is no striking investment in the bazaars or shop displays, etc., no pretensions to luxury in any of the fixtures. The only amenities are apt to be brilliant lighting or a radio-phonograph. Bazaars definitely do not contribute to the charm of Lima streets.[29] Their profits are also hardly noticeable. In marked contrast to the well-to-do people of Spanish descent, Japanese business people, some of whom are very prosperous, are not ostentatious. Some of them have bought good cotton land, hold shares in industrial enterprises (manufacturing silk stockings, cheap hats, etc.), or own "hotels." Prac-

[28] These figures are considered to be reasonable by one familiar with the trade.
[29] The *Asociación Nacional Pro-Marina* pointed out that Japanese do not build like other foreign colonists do, and that their shops always look "provisional" (letter to *La Prensa*, August 29, 1937). Another contributor lamented that the existence of Japanese bazaars prevented the establishment of big department stores in Lima (*ibid.*, August 31, 1937).

tically none of them lives in the attractive new houses around Lima, and several inhabit the buildings in which they work. None of them goes about in "society" or is seen in expensive places of amusement. It is safe to assume that they save a large part of their profits which they probably remit to Japan.

Accusations, so often levelled against both large and small merchants, of being sharp and of taking part in disreputable contraband transactions or fraudulent activities—as charged in Parliament in September 1941 against two of the larger firms—are probably gross exaggerations. Without making a point of being extraordinarily scrupulous when confronted with an attractive offer, the heads of Japanese bazaars are generally sufficiently responsible to avoid shady business deals. Their reputation for fulfilling obligations is of course excellent, as is their credit rating (with one or two exceptions).

In addition to the bazaars, the Japanese engage in only a few other branches of retail trade.[30] A few stationery shops and a comparatively high proportion of the total number of small shops selling staple food articles (sometimes consumed on the premises) practically exhaust the list. However, Japanese enjoy a virtual monopoly as hairdressers and barbers,[31] and

[30] In several cases Japanese displaced Chinese. Peruvians did not attempt to enter the field, because of their "national" dislike of such trades (Salinas Cossio, *La Prensa,* Oct. 19, 1937). Chinese have fully maintained their position as butchers. The diminutive coffee and tea shops appear to be a Japanese invention, absorbing elements from previous Chinese and Italian types of similar institutions.

[31] Close considered the presence of Japanese barbers in the Panama Canal Zone to be extremely suspicious: "déja plusieurs centaines de

they predominate among the tiny coffee and tea shops, where at all hours cheap food and doubtful drinks can be had for a trifle. Possibly three-quarters of the more than 200 such shops in Lima are owned by Japanese. And most of them, according to a high Peruvian authority, utilize their well-attended shops as meeting-places, information exchanges and centers of influence.[32]

Related to this trade is the preparation of *chicha* (fermented maize). Because chicha is a popular and distinctively "national" drink, this is one of the most commonly resented of all of the Japanese activities in Peru.[33] For similar reasons, there are misgivings about the comparatively high number of Japanese bakeries and shops selling local, highly-spiced specialties. In Lima they are as numerous as those owned by Peruvians. In the public markets, periodical fairs, and among street peddlers, Japanese represent almost 20 per cent of the total in Lima, while Peruvians constitute 55 per cent and Chinese 12 per cent.

---

boutiques de coiffeurs japonais s'alignent le long des écluses" (*op. cit.*, p. 474). Ease of movement and personal cleanliness are probably two points in favor of Japanese as barbers. On November 7 and 8, 1941, the newspapers reported the adoption of certain restrictions by the Government of the Republic of Panama, which were resented by the Japanese as being discriminatory.

[32] "El japonés, sobre todo el dueño de pulpería o de tambo, hace de su negocio un centro de concurrencia, de información y de influjo" (Ulloa, *op. cit.*, p. 347).

[33] "Hasta la fabricación de productos netamentes nacionales, como la chicha, pertenece a los japoneses" (Zegarra, E. "El Fomento de las Industrias y el Capital Extranjero," *La Nueva Economia*, April 1941, p. 107). Gonzales Tello (*La Prensa,* Oct. 14, 1937) asked the municipalities to investigate the foods and drinks "que los japoneses venden para intoxicar al pueblo." A recent decree (October 23, 1941) established new "sanitary" restrictions for the *chicha* and *jora* industries.

Almost a quarter of the mechanical and watch-making and -repairing shops in Lima are run by Japanese. The proportion is probably higher among the glass-cutters and picture-frame makers, and also among plumbers and sanitary engineers. In Lima *japonés* is a synonym of *gasfitero*,[34] just as *chino* is synonymous with "drugstore." Less important but still sizable is the proportion of Japanese in the subsidiary electrical and automobile trades (battery making and repairing, tire repairing and reconstructing, tin-plating and painting).

In sum, Japanese constitute a good proportion among skilled workers in Lima. The Peruvian authority cited above admitted that the Japanese worker is generally preferred because he is often cheaper and "much more painstaking and conscientious" than the Peruvian.[35] Their role in large- and medium-scale industry is far less important.[36] A hat factory (with an annual production of some ten to twelve thousand dozen felt and straw hats and berets), a small omnibus enterprise, one or two cotton-ginning plants, and cottonseed-oil mills in Chancay Valley—that is about all.

[34] *Gasfitero* (English "gasfitter") is a phonetic transliteration similar to *futbol* and *beisbol*.
[35] "Mucho más cumplido y concienzudo en su labor" (Ulloa, *op. cit.*, p. 348).
[36] According to Mr. Aiba, then Japanese Consul-General in Lima, the following were in 1911 the occupations of Japanese in Peru: 77 small traders, 69 restaurant keepers, 45 grocers, 54 carpenters, 19 coal venders and 30 to 40 factory hands. (Martin, *op. cit.*, p. 126.) According to Toru Ogishima (quoted by Salinas Cossio, *La Prensa*, Oct. 19, 1937), there were in Peru in 1934 only 452 Japanese engaged in industry, as against 4,773 in commerce and 1,899 in agriculture. "Commerce" probably includes independent artisans.

Among its customers the Banco Industrial includes (1941) 62 foreigners, of 16 different nationalities, as against 172 Peruvians. But although the Japanese is the largest foreign colony in the country, not a single Japanese is listed among the borrowers from this bank.

There, are, however, some signs of growing interest in industry. A wholesale dealer in Japanese and other imported drugs has inaugurated the industrial exploitation of some Peruvian raw products; a textile importer has established a shirt factory; at least two bazaar owners and importers are interested in a plant manufacturing lady's stockings and characteristically called *Fábrica Nacional de Medias "El Inca"*; and an enterprising owner of small restaurants is trying to enter the field of aerated waters, syrups and popular-priced liquors. Thus there appears to be a tendency toward a modest "vertical" integration of productive activities. The most effective deterrent is probably the strong inclination of the Japanese to go back home "some day," and his consequent reluctance to sink deep roots elsewhere. A bazaar can be liquidated in a few weeks' time and, as a matter of fact, is actually liquidated through sales three or four times a year. An industrial plant is not so easily disposed of.

III. TRADE WITH JAPAN

General Characteristics

The chief characteristic of trade between Peru and Japan since the first World War has been the lack of balance between the export and import trends. Peruvian exports to Japan were very small for many years (generally less than half of one per cent of total

TRADE OF PERU WITH JAPAN
(in soles)

Year	Imports	Per cent of Total Imports	Exports	Per cent of Total Exports
1918	2,730,350	2.8	692,640	0.3
1921	2,784,903	1.7	1,154,560	0.7
1925	1,891,050	1.0	608,830	0.3
1928	2,006,010	1.2	1,458,600	0.5
1931	1,654,906	1.6	24,500	...
1932	1,259,718	1.6	37,400	...
1933	5,277,369	4.9	999,190	0.4
1934	10,225,602	6.0	5,084,536	1.7
1935	9,392,426	5.2	8,890,230	2.9
1936	7,874,121	3.9	14,060,244	4.2
1937	8,105,241	3.4	3,887,083	1.1
1938	8,683,775	3.3	1,952,374	0.6
1939	8,016,479	3.1	9,110,727	2.4
1940	18,570,071	5.8	31,613,132	7.8
1941	15,903,803	4.4	82,239,883	16.6

exports). During the depression years of the early 1930's they declined almost to nothing and then rose rapidly in the year of the abrogation of the Treaty of

Commerce (1934). Their subsequent course was very irregular, sinking in 1938 to little more than half of one per cent, only to jump to about eight per cent at the outbreak of the second World War and to 20.8 per cent in the first half of 1941.

TRADE BETWEEN JAPAN AND PERU
(thousand soles)

Average exchange for one yen	Year	Exports from Peru to Japan — Japanese Statistics	Exports from Peru to Japan — Peruvian Statistics	Imports from Japan to Peru — Japanese Statistics	Imports from Japan to Peru — Peruvian Statistics
1.31	1934	2,388.1	5,084.5	9,011.4	10,225.6
1.21	1935	13,812.1	8,890,2	8,422.8	9,392.4
1.17	1936	15,210.0	14,060.2	7,202.5	7,874.1
1.15	1937	7,218.5	3,887.1	7,295.6	8,105.2
1.27	1938	2,508.2	1,952.4	7,315.2	8,683.8
1.43	1939	9,947.1	9,110.7	8,700.1	8,016.5

The import (from Japan to Peru) figures agree very closely. The wide differences in the export figures may be due to Japanese purchases of Peruvian cotton in Liverpool (when Peruvian figures are higher) to declarations below the real value made by Peruvian exporters (when their figures are lower), and to other factors.

Imports from Japan, on the other hand, remained between one and two per cent of total imports all through the post-war and depression years, rising, at the time of the big Japanese export drive, to a steady three to four per cent (and even more in the years when the Government was buying armaments in Japan). Imports from Japan rose after the outbreak of the war (1940-41), but they failed to keep pace with the rocket-like rise in exports (of cotton) to Japan. In the first half of 1941 their percentage of total imports returned to the more normal figure of 4.85 per cent.[1]

[1] Imports fell off in 1941 perhaps because, after the riots of May 1940, the bazaars carried smaller stocks of goods. In the Japanese statistics the Peruvian percentage is even lower, varying (during 1934-39) between 0.1 and 0.5 per cent.

The composition of exports to and imports from Japan differed markedly. Exports comprised a very few raw commodities; imports, a multitude of foods, textiles, and other manufactured articles. This difference, of course, characterizes Peruvian foreign trade in general, but it was particularly noticeable in the case of trade with Japan. In fact, in certain years Peruvian exports to Japan were represented by only one or two items, whereas imports numbered several hundred.[2] The difficulties and uncertainties of Peruvian foreign commerce were greatest in the trade with Japan, and it is not astonishing that treaties have been without result (as that of 1873) or short-lived (as that of 1928, which was denounced in 1934).

Exports [3]

During the whole 1919-41 period the most constant export articles were alpaca (and to a much

[2] Japanese imports into Peru, few of which are heavy goods or articles favored by tariff exemption or low rates, paid comparatively high duties. In 1939 duties on Japanese imports totalled 2,969,426 soles, i.e., 37% *ad valorem*. No other country with sizable imports paid so much, with the exception of rice-exporting countries (Thailand, Ecuador), because of the high protective tariff on rice.

[3] In this investigation of Peruvian trade with Japan, the author examined all Peruvian Foreign Trade Yearbooks since 1919, and concerned himself only with items (both exports and imports) with a declared value exceeding 20,000 soles. This method has certain obvious defects: (1) the figure of 20,000 soles does not represent a fixed real value, since the value of the sole has not remained constant. (2) Customs classification of goods has changed from time to time, thus not only shifting certain items from one category to another but also sub-dividing and re-grouping items in new ways. (3) As much as from five to ten per cent of imports are classed under such unenlightening headings as "other items," "items not classified," etc. (4) No account is taken of the relative importance of the trade in the same articles with other (non-Japanese) countries; yet it makes a considerable difference whether imports from Japan of a certain item, amounting to, say, 20,000 soles, represents the entire Peruvian imports

lesser extent sheep and llama) wool. This amounts to an important sum every year, with the exception of the crisis (1929-30) and early war (1939-40) years. Since alpaca wool is an almost exclusive Peruvian monopoly, this stability is not surprising. Japan competed for purchases of alpaca wool with England, and in later years also with the United States and Germany.

Cotton exports followed a completely different pattern. They were important in the years immediately following the first World War, and then disappeared almost completely until 1933. Thereafter, Japan was a regular buyer,[4] though the size of its purchases varied considerably from one year to another. Ikeyama has said that the decline was due to the negligence of Peruvian exporters, who are neither Peruvians nor Japanese, and declared that Japan "is always ready to buy any amount of Peruvian cotton."[5]

---

of that item or only a small percentage. (5) Even in its annotated form, the tabular summary (more than 125 columns long) gives almost as much prominence to an import worth 20,001 soles as to one worth, say, a million. Notwithstanding these weaknesses, the data reveal certain general trends, which are discussed in the text. It is worth noting that traffic in contraband goods, which is considerable, does not of course appear in the official data.

[4] According to Ikeyama ("Acerca del Comercio Peruano-Japonés," *La Prensa*, Oct. 12, 1937), until 1934 Japanese mill owners had no idea of the high quality of Peruvian cotton. When they noticed that they bought little from Peru, whereas their sales were rising so rapidly that quotas were being imposed on their imports, they determined to buy more, and started with cotton—all of which looks like an explanation after the fact and an attempt to trade cotton purchases for textile import quotas. On the next day Ikeyama (*ibid.*, Oct. 13, 1937) wrote significantly: "Un país no adquiere algodón por capricho o filantropía sino obedeciendo a exigencias industriales," and hinted shrewdly at the possibility of Japan's also buying oil, sugar, wool, etc.

[5] "Está siempre dispuesto a comprar cualquier cantidad de algodón peruano" (*ibid.*, Oct. 15, 1937).

After the outbreak of the second World War Japan became the leading purchaser of Peruvian cotton, making good to a large extent the loss of former European markets. In 1940 its purchases totalled 21.2 million soles, and in the first eight months of 1941 no less than 60 million, thus rescuing the cotton growers from disaster and incidentally helping to dispel the recent wave of anti-Japanese feeling. The outbreak of war in the Pacific and subsequent events cut off a valuable outlet upon which Peru might normally have become increasingly dependent. Nevertheless, it is significant that Japan was hard pressed to pay for its big 1941 imports of Peruvian cotton. Toward the end of September a Japanese ship brought gold to Callao, a rare import in the land of Inca gold.

Cocaine was another regular article of export until 1929, at which time it ceased abruptly, probably as a result of the suspension of activity by the Japanese-owned cocaine plant in Huanuco. Tagua, coffee, and sugar are among the other subtropical products occasionally exported to Japan. But of much greater significance was the export of minerals, which was considerably developed and diversified in 1939 and 1940. Whereas previously only copper ores (in 1928 and 1938), crude petroleum (1928), gasoline (1934), and electrolytic lead from the La Oroya plant (1937-38) had been sent to Japan in appreciable quantities,[6] Japan bought lead concentrates and tungsten ores in

[6] By United States firms, since the petroleum and gasoline probably came from Talara (the International Petroleum Company, a subsidiary of the Standard Oil Company), and the copper and lead from La Oroya (the Cerro de Pasco Copper Corporation).

1939, and also molybdenum concentrates and antimonium and vanadium ores in 1940. Nonetheless, these mineral shipments, as well as those of common salt and lead exported in 1941,[7] remained comparatively small, and the "inter-American" legislation enacted in June and July of 1941 halted them completely.

Imports

As early as the first post-war years, Japan exported certain kinds of cheap textiles to Peru—such as gray goods and stockings, shirts and trousers, camisoles, and various silk goods. These shipments, never very important, were accompanied by a stream of typical foods (dried fish, canned crabmeat, dried mushrooms and vegetables, small lobsters and other shellfish, seeds and cereals, etc.), toys, glassware, porcelain and hardware articles. Imports were, therefore, intended for consumption by the local Japanese colony, and also by the poorer members of the Peruvian population. A small amount (some silk goods and certain of the more expensive food specialties) was in demand by the wealthier sections of both.

Towards 1925 the character of Japanese imports changed. Porcelain and glassware were eliminated by competition from Czechoslovakian manufacturers. Certain textiles and the cheaper toilet goods suffered an eclipse, while a few foodstuffs decreased sharply. At the same time there appeared new items which

[7] A total of 1,700 tons of Huacho salt was bought, at U. S. $2.36 per ton, and exported by the Fuji Trading Company (*Revista de Hacienda*, No. 5, 1941, pp. 60-1). Some 461 tons of lead and silver concentrates were exported to Japan in May (see Ministerial Resolution of May 9, 1941, in *Boletín de Aduanas*, XIX (1941), p. 257).

were to continue until 1941—buttons, toothbrushes, handkerchiefs, table and bed linen, toilet articles, black percale—articles which heralded the appearance of the bazaars. This trend continued throughout the depression.

A new phase began in 1931-32, with the devaluation of the yen and the big Japanese export drive,[8] which coincided with a marked decline in the purchasing power of the Peruvian people. All textile imports increased; new as well as traditional food articles flooded the market; some chemical products, such as insecticides, appeared for the first time. In 1933 the Government made important purchases of war materials in Japan. In the same year Japanese imports of glassware and hardware reappeared in force. The trend was definitely upward. The denunciation in 1934 of the Treaty of Commerce did little to counteract it. More effective was the quota on Japanese textiles. Between 1934 and 1939 annual imports were steady at between eight and ten million soles, but diversification increased until imports of textiles, for example, included high-quality as well as cheap goods, rayon and woolen articles in addition to cotton and silk, and cot-

---

[8] According to Condliffe, J. B. (*The Reconstruction of World Trade,* New York, 1940, p. 228), this drive was due mainly to a "national policy of credit expansion correlated with war expenditures and protected by the fall of the exchange rate," and helped by new techniques and plenty of cheap labor. Japanese competition in Peru is mentioned for the first time in several years in the British Department of Overseas Trade *Report on Economic Conditions in Peru* for 1931 (pp. 83-84) and the 1934 Report stresses the huge increase (over 150 per cent in 1933 over 1932) in imports of Japanese cotton textiles and mentions the special facilities and easy credit offered by Japanese firms (pp. 12-13).

ton yarns and artificial fibers as well as finished articles and clothing.

This variety was even more striking in the other types of imports. In addition to maintaining their positions in the glassware, hardware and food trades, Japanese penetrated dozens of new fields. The most striking development was the increase in imports of such Japanese manufactures as agricultural machinery, bicycles, automobile tires, rubber and celluloid goods, batteries, automobile parts and accessories, electric-light bulbs, flashlights, watches, cement, gramophones and records, metal appliances and buttons, etc. Many of these articles are not sold in bazaars; almost all of them are lower in price than American or even German manufactures. If, as seems likely, this recent Japanese export drive reached a hitherto untouched consumer group, its effects were of course more important for the Peruvian than for the Japanese economy.

Peru's trade with Japan was abnormal in 1940, and even more so in 1941. Several of the items imported for the first time in these years (sheet iron, tin-plate, metal spoons and forks, thermos bottles, electrical switchboards, chemical dyes, paper goods, tools, etc.) made their appearance as a result of the dislocation of normal trade channels by the war. Japanese goods did not compete with such popular American articles as automobiles, radios, refrigerators, chemical and pharmaceutical products. Nor did Japan offer capital goods such as rails and railway equipment, industrial machinery, and the like. But in almost every other field Japanese manufactures enjoyed notable success in the Peruvian market, for they are cheap and have the advantage of a complete Japanese distribution network within the country. As the largest buyer of Peruvian cotton, Japan was in a good bargaining position to seek favorable treatment and the removal of discriminatory legislation or unfriendly propaganda against its products.

Other Items in the Balance of Payments

Very little is known about these "other items." Government expenditures abroad were included in the general trade statistics until at least 1935, but not since 1938 or possibly earlier. In any case, it is unlikely that a substantial part of the 26 million soles spent abroad by the government in 1938 and 1939 for munitions [9] was spent in Japan. Shipping and insurance were completely passive items in the Peruvian balance of payments. Japanese ships carried almost all of the trade between the two countries.[10]

[9] *Revista de Hacienda*, No. 1, p. 27. In 1938 the "Aprovisionamientos del Estado" amounted to 16,154,660 soles (*ibid.*, pp. 32-3), and in 1939 to 9,839,221 soles (*ibid.*, No. 4, pp. 421-2). In 1940 such expenses amounted to only 832,000 soles (*ibid.*, 1941, No. 8, p. 461).

[10] During the last more or less normal years, the goods carried by Japanese ships do not seem to have increased appreciably.

Year	Total foreign ships entering Peruvian ports Number	Tonnage (000)	Japanese ships entering Peruvian ports Number	Tonnage (000)	Japanese ships as percentage of total Number	Tonnage (000)
1937	4,401	13,973.1	178	845.9	4.0	6.1
1938	4,216	13,549.5	127	643.6	3.0	4.7
1939	3,984	12,597.3	199	998.8	5.0	7.9
1940	2,654	7,737.1	152	740.2	5.7	9.6

Japanese ships have long enjoyed large government subsidies. Salinas Cossio stated that Japanese freight rates were 25% lower than those of

It is likely that the Japanese colony remits to Japan a considerable portion of their savings, which, as noted above, constitute a substantial part of their earnings. There are no comprehensive data on this movement; records of bank purchases and sales of yen, or even of Hongkong dollars, provide a very incomplete picture of the situation.

PERUVIAN BANK TRANSACTIONS IN YEN AND
HONGKONG DOLLARS
(In thousands)

	Japanese yen			Hongkong dollars		
Year	Bought	Sold	Excess of sales	Bought	Sold	Excess of sales
1936	129.4	4,710.4	4,581.0	36.1	4,658.8	4,622.7
1937	181.5	4,470.6	4,289.0	131.2	4,630.2	4,499.0
1938	163.0	2,966.6	2,803.6	242.4	2,519.2	2,276.8
1939	121.3	2,260.3	2,139.0	102.0	2,995.5	2,893.5
1940	1,033.4	2,950.0	1,916.6	1,859.1	4,484.0	2,624.9

Another important part of the outward flow was undoubtedly represented by remittances of U. S. dollars and, in former years, of pounds sterling. Other payments were also made to unofficial agents of Japanese banks.[11] International postal money orders were not much employed for this purpose.

---

any other nation (*La Prensa*, Sept. 28, 1937). Pearsall, Charles H. J., "Transportation Problems," *The Annals*, Vol. 204 (1939), p. 161, reports the comparatively small sum of 16,000 dollars as the subsidy received by the Nippon Yusen Kaisha for its services to the American west coast. According to *Chunambei* (Latin America), a publication of the Japanese Federation of the Associations of Traders with Latin America (Osaka, 1939-40, p. 104), the South American west coast was served by four N.Y.K. ships (totalling 34,681 tons) and by four Kawasaki Kisen Kaisha ships (34,136 tons).

[11] Japanese banks have no branches in Peru, nor has the Japanese colony founded a bank of its own there.

Considered as a whole, the total stream must have been of considerable importance. All that Ikeyama could say by way of minimizing it was that such sums sent to families in Japan were "very modest ones, especially if they are compared with those sent out by other foreign colonies." [12] Nevertheless, in view also of the absence of data on Japanese capital movements (investments, withdrawals, liquidations, etc.), any attempt at estimating a balance of payments must be considered misleading.

[12] Ikeyama, "Nuevos conceptos sobre los mismos errores," *La Prensa*, Oct. 24, 1937.

IV. ANTI-JAPANESE LEGISLATION

Peru has passed no laws or regulations specifically intended to limit or control Japanese activities within its borders. But in two significant respects general regulations have been so devised and administered that they have affected the Japanese particularly.[1] The first group of measures limits Japanese immigration into Peru, in order to protect the "racial homogeneity" of the Peruvian people. The second imposes a quota upon imports of Japanese textiles,[2] with the twofold purpose of protecting Peru's largest domestic industry and pleasing the textile manufacturers of Great Britain, which was until recently the leading buyer of Peruvian cotton.

Immigration Restrictions

The law respecting immigration and the activities of foreigners in Peru (June 26, 1936) does not mention Japanese, or even Asiatics. But since there is no other "foreign group" to which its intentions and

[1] The law (of November 29, 1940) compelling foreign newspapers in Lima, printed in type other than roman, to publish a parallel translation of the text in Castilian, was probably dictated by the same anti-Oriental bias.

[2] "S" lamented that the textile quota was the *only* restriction against Japanese infiltration (*La Prensa*, Aug. 31, 1937).

rulings could apply,[3] there can be no doubt about its purpose.

Any possible doubt was dispelled by the frank explanation of A. Ulloa, the author of the law, who disclosed that, when he was Minister of Foreign Affairs under President Benavides, the latter had been urged by various people to take strong measures against the Japanese. Rumors were then current to the effect that important persons were illegally implicated in the toleration of Japanese immigration and infiltration in Peru. Benavides and Ulloa therefore decided to institute restrictive measures. These had to be severe because of the seriousness of the Japanese menace. They had to be general because it would have been unusual, from the point of view of international law, to enforce them exclusively against Japanese. And finally they had to be drawn up in secrecy because of possible complications abroad and also in Peru, where certain Peruvian interests would be affected. No one but Benavides and Ulloa knew anything about them until they had signed the decree; then, after submission to the Cabinet, which gave its enthusiastic approval, the decree was immediately published.[4]

[3] Moreyra y Paz Soldan, Carlos, *La Prensa,* Aug. 29, 1937; and Salinas Cossio, *ibid.,* Oct. 19, 1937.
[4] Ulloa, *op. cit.,* pp. 349-51. Of interest also is the account of the protests, activities and intrigues of the Japanese Minister Murakami, who tried to obtain the revocation, suspension, or at least the modification of the regulations—without appreciable success (*ibid.,* pp. 356-9). Further details may be found in the note of Foreign Minister de la Fuente to the Japanese *chargé d'affaires* on August 14, 1937. The note denied the existence of anti-Japanese discrimination, but concluded: "La opinión pública del Perú ha ido viendo con alarma creciente como, mediante métodos de trabajo y condiciones individuales que les son peculiares, los súbditos japoneses han desplazado sucesivamente al elemento nacional de una

The law seeks to deal with certain abuses in which Oriental, and especially Japanese, immigrants are commonly supposed to engage. These undesirable activities are encouraged by the "nationalistic tendencies" of certain countries which continue to supervise the behavior of their nationals even after they have emigrated abroad. This practice has created competition for Peruvian laborers and tradespeople who have become uneasy owing to the increasing influence of the immigrants in their adopted country. The Peruvian Government held that monopolies, which are forbidden by the Constitution, must be interpreted as including the exclusive or predominant exploitation of any field of activity, "as is the case in certain industries and trades." [5]

The law restricts immigration to 16,000 persons of any one nationality (thereby fixing a limit which the Japanese exceeded). It forbids the immigration of organized "racial groups" (this affecting only Orientals). And it extends to all professions, trades and arts, and also to the yanacones,[6] in every province, the obli-

---

serie de actividades en las cuales predominaba como número y como capital" ("Immigración y actividades de los japoneses en el Perú," *Boletín del Ministerio de Relaciones Exteriores*, XXXIV, 1937, No. 129, pp. 178-86). Was it simply a coincidence that the *La Prensa* campaign, described above, started just a week later?

[5] Ulloa granted that it was a most delicate task ("uno de los trabajos más delicados") to insert the desired regulations without coming into conflict with the Constitution (*op. cit.*, p. 351).

[6] It is permissible to transfer a farm from one *yanacon* to another of the same nationality, when no Peruvian is interested in obtaining the farm. It is commonly claimed that neither this regulation nor the main one, regarding the 20% limit on the employment of foreigners, is observed. (See the debate in the Senate, *El Comercio*, Aug. 27, 1940, and in the Chamber of Deputies, *ibid.*, Nov. 8, 1941.)

gation of employers to engage a personnel that is at least 80 per cent Peruvian—a regulation which originally affected only commercial and industrial enterprises. Other regulations give ample freedom of restrictive action to the Ministry of Foreign Relations, which may provide "special instructions" to Peruvian consuls abroad.

Recently additional measures were instituted to avoid the danger of "double nationality." In this case, too, the motive was clearly anti-Japanese. By an act of July 31, 1940, persons born in Peru of foreign parents belonging to countries observing the *jus sanguinis*, who during their minority leave Peru for their parents' homeland, to live, study or undergo military training there, automatically lose their Peruvian citizenship, and, until their citizenship is restored, must be considered as "alien immigrants." [7] In September 1940 the Chamber of Deputies debated and approved a still more restrictive law which provided that the sons of foreigners, even if born in Peru, are during their minority to be considered as being of the same nationality as their fathers.[8] These regulations were commented on by the President in his 1941 message to Congress in a way which plainly referred to the Japanese colony.[9]

[7] *El Comercio,* Aug. 6, 1940.
[8] *Ibid.,* Sept. 5, 13, 14, 19, 20 and 21, 1940.
[9] "Existen en nuestro país colonias de extranjeros en donde los menores de edad, nacidos en nuestro territorio, son considerados nominalmente peruanos, solo para los efectos de burlar las cuotas o los impuestos de extranjería, estando, en realidad, estrechamente vinculados a la patria de sus padres y sojetidos directamente a la jurisdicción de las respectivos Gobiernos extranjeros" (*Mensaje presentado al Congreso,* etc., Official Edition, Lima, 1941, p. 24).

Trade Restrictions

The quota on imports of textiles was first imposed on May 10, 1935, and applied to goods regardless of their origin, on the ground that "foreign" textiles had invaded the Peruvian markets, endangering domestic mills and causing unemployment. The failure to mention Japan specifically may have been due to the fact that the Treaty of Commerce was at that time still in operation.[10] But the monthly *Bulletin* of the Lima Chamber of Commerce did not mince matters: "As is well known, the real purpose of this Decree has been to stop Japanese imports."[11]

Domestic prices were frozen, and quotas fixed, but only the Japanese quota (204,238 kilograms for the half-year beginning June 1) represented a really restrictive instrument. Before the expiration of this period, on October 11, 1935, an influential group of importers, both Japanese and non-Japanese, asked that the quota be limited to articles manufactured in Peru (or about 75 of the 167 cotton-goods items listed in the Customs Tariff). This request was supported by both the Chamber of Commerce and the *Sociedad Nacional de Industrias*.[12]

The government at first directed that the quota system be continued, and insisted that the Japanese accept transformation of the quota into a freely accepted limitation. When the Japanese refused to do

---

[10] Such is the explanation given by Salinas Cossio, *La Prensa,* Sept. 23, 1937.
[11] *Boletín de la Cámara de Comercio de Lima,* VI (1935), pp. 202-3.
[12] *Ibid.,* pp. 483-5.

so,[13] a special Decree was issued (December 30, 1935), changing the whole system substantially. The quota was then made openly anti-Japanese, but 47 (and later 50) tariff items were put on the free list, and the Japanese quota was increased 50 per cent (to 612,714 kilograms annually). This arrangement was described as a temporary step, pending the completion of a new agreement between Peru and Japan.[14]

These measures were short-lived, but they paved the way for the agreement reached on March 24, 1936, between the Japanese diplomatic representative in Lima and the Peruvian Government—an agreement which in the main was still being observed in November 1941. The Japanese agreed voluntarily to limit their cotton-goods exports (excepting the 50 items not manufactured in Peru, and also exports destined for the Amazon Department of Loreto) to an annual quota of 612,714 kilograms. A further agreement between the Japanese Consulate and the Commercial Department of the Peruvian Ministry of Foreign Affairs established that 70 per cent of such imports was to be bought by Japanese importers and the remaining 30 per cent by non-Japanese. This latter provision aroused the Chamber of Commerce, which attacked the "unfortunate precedent" of discrimination according to the nationality of tradespeople, but the protests went unheeded. The new arrangement served to strengthen the control of the Japanese authorities over their

[13] For the official communique, see *ibid.*, VII (1936), p. 162.
[14] *Ibid.*, pp. 4-5. In its Yearly Report for 1935, the Chamber of Commerce noted with satisfaction that the quota system had given "los resultados apetecidos" (*ibid.*, p. 62).

nationals, since the import licenses had now to be approved by the Japanese Consulate in Lima, and then forwarded through the Peruvian Foreign Ministry to the Peruvian consuls in Kobe and Yokohama.[15]

Toward the end of 1936 the Chamber asked for a revision of the agreement in favor of non-Japanese importers.[16] However, no change was made when the first year of the agreement expired. It was renewed for another six months, with some important items (stockings and handkerchiefs) being added to the free list.[17] Finally, on September 23, 1937, when the quota agreement was extended to December 31, 1938, the non-Japanese importers obtained 50 per cent (instead of their previous 30 per cent) of the quota.[18]

Because of difficulties in Japan, the 1938 quota was not filled.[19] Nevertheless on November 30, 1938, the Japanese Minister in Lima requested an increase in the quota to 1,000 or at least 850 tons annually, in addition to new exemptions. In return he offered a preferential market in Japan for Peruvian cotton. Both the Chamber of Commerce and the *Sociedad*

[15] *Ibid.*, p. 164.
[16] *Ibid.*, pp. 668-9. Another request was made by the non-Japanese importers on April 14, 1937 (*ibid.*, VIII, pp. 172-3), whereupon the Ministry promised to study the possibility of their securing a better share of the quota (*ibid.*, p. 239).
[17] *Ibid.*, VIII (1937), pp. 171-2.
[18] *Ibid.*, p. 529. The Japanese repeated their request for the abolition of this unfriendly measure as speedily as possible. From an exchange of notes published in the *Boletín del Ministerio de Relaciones Exteriores* (XXXIV, 1937, pp. 194-203), it appears that they first requested 60% of the quota before accepting (on September 10, 1937) the fifty-fifty arrangement, at which time they asked for a higher quota. They also insisted, without success, on having the quota restricted to such articles as competed with Peruvian-manufactured ones.
[19] *Boletín de la Cámara de Comercio de Lima*, IX (1938), pp. 561-2.

Nacional de Industrias considered the Japanese demands unacceptable [20] on the grounds that not even the current quota had been filled, and that other countries would protest if Japan received preferential treatment.

The retention of the previous quota [21] was in part due to British pressure. After the outbreak of war in 1939, the British (according to certain rumors) insisted that they could continue to buy Peruvian products (mainly cotton) only if the quota on Japanese imports were maintained. They declared that the Treaty of Commerce between Peru and Great Britain had been signed by them on this understanding.[22] In their effort to take the place of the Germans, forcibly excluded from the Peruvian market, the English found it necessary to guard against the possibility of Germany's exports being replaced by those of Japanese make. The quota was, therefore, no longer a bone of contention between Japanese and Peruvian mills. It had become (or possibly it stood revealed as what it

[20] *Ibid.*, pp. 667-9.

[21] No official document was published at that time. Towards the end of 1939 arrangements were made to remove shipping difficulties and to distribute the 1940 quota (*ibid.*, X (1939), pp. 570-2). The same silence was observed at the end of 1940 (*ibid.*, XI, pp. 614-15). But in his Presidential Message of July 28, 1941, President Prado said that the agreement had been extended during 1941 (Official Edition, Lima, 1941, p. 25).

[22] This was substantially true. The British agreed to open the negotiations for the Treaty only after the first quota decree had been published ("Report of the Peruvian Commercial Mission to the Peruvian Foreign Minister, May 15, 1936," *Boletín de la Cámara de Comercio de Lima*, VII (1936), p. 480). Among the arguments against an increase in the quota, the Secretary of the Chamber of Commerce suggested that it could "perjudicar nuestras relaciones comerciales con países en los que el Perú encuentra mercados seguros para sus productos"—an obvious reference to Great Britain (*ibid.*, IX (1938), p. 668).

ANTI-JAPANESE LEGISLATION 121

had been from the very beginning) an episode in the commercial contest between England on the one hand and Germany and Japan on the other.[23]

[23] After the outbreak of hostilities between Japan and the United States, the Peruvian Government froze the accounts and holdings of Japanese citizens in Peru. Unofficially it was explained that such measures were definitely not of a political, but of an economic, character and were intended to guarantee the compliance of Japanese with their commercial obligations. The same measures were not to be extended to Italian and German nationals resident in Peru.

The Japanese Consulate allowed publication in the Lima papers of a prominent advertisement, recommending Japanese residents to observe an "actitud prudente y tranquila," to abstain from unnecessary travels or meetings, and to refrain from comments on politics and war. It was also officially declared by the Japanese Government that they had frozen no South American funds (*El Comercio*, December 16, 1941). On January 6, 1942, the Peruvian Foreign Minister declared that the importance of the Japanese problem in Peru had been exaggerated: "the influence of the Japanese colony"—he said—"is insignificant, as they are mostly retailers" (*El Comercio*, January 7, 1942). On May 9, 1942, President Prado, interviewed by newspaper men in Washington about "the danger of a Japanese fifth column in Peru" minimized it, "declaring the situation under control" (*New York Times*, May 10, 1942). The "Proclaimed List of Certain Blocked Nationals" (American Blacklist) in Revision II, May 12, 1942; Suppl. 1, May 22, 1942; and Suppl. 2, June 2, 1942, includes about 566 Japanese firms established in Peru, in a total of 859 blocked firms. (Almost all the 293 non-Japanese firms are German.)

Public opinion towards Japanese remains rather hostile, but not to the point of boycotting Japanese shops or artisans. Many cheap Japanese articles have already disappeared from the market. The hardest blow to Japanese interests, however, was dealt by the law No. 9592 (June 26, 1942), which, in view also of the recent agreements with the United States about cotton and other Peruvian export crops, orders the annulment of all contracts of land-leasing (*yanacones*, etc.) when the leaser is blacklisted, and the transference of the land to a Peruvian by birth (i.e., not a nationalized one). Analogous measures are dictated for the "blacklisted" businesses, either commercial, industrial or mining. The list of the properties affected was to be published by decree. The "Superintendencia de Economía" is in charge of the administrative steps and procedure.

V. CONCLUSION

The ordinary Peruvian knows that most Japanese are ready to sacrifice themselves for their fatherland.[1] He knows that they are all imbued with the traditional ideals of fanatical patriotism and devotion to the Emperor. And, therefore, even while he respects and even admires the individual Japanese—as a good worker, successful shopkeeper, or skilled mechanic— he regards with misgivings such a stand-offish and organized foreign group—people who do not speak Castilian, do not profess the Catholic faith, do not attempt to participate in the social and intellectual life of the country, and send their money away. To many Peruvians Japanese tenacity and diligence seem doubly dangerous.

This dislike, usually latent but sometimes violent, contains the customary elements of the reaction provoked in a living organism, such as the body politic is,

[1] So does the ex-Minister for Foreign Affairs, Mr. Ulloa. He describes vividly (*op. cit.*, pp. 360-2) the possible dangers to the Panama Canal defenses from a Japanese landing on the deserted and indefensible coast of Peru. Among strategic objectives in Peru he mentions the Talara oilfields, the Chicama sugar-cane fields, the port of Callao with its dry-dock and railway leading to the Sierra mining districts, and Mollendo with its railway to the Titicaca and Bolivia. Twenty thousand Japanese in Peru "estarían en una beligerancia activa o virtual contra los Estados Unidos y contra nuestro propio país, aliado natural, en la política o [y?] en el espíritu, de la gran nación del Norte."

CONCLUSION 123

by the introduction of another, smaller organism which continues to live its own life—suspicion, irritation, impatience, and the like. But, added to these, it contains more specific elements, such as the knowledge that the smaller intrusive organism is a part of an enormously larger one with dangerous tendencies. In other words, to the ordinary reasonable Peruvian, the Japanese "danger" does not lie in Lima, nor even in Chancay, but in Tokyo.[2]

Note has been made of the coincidence between the last great anti-Japanese agitation and the start of the Sino-Japanese war in 1937. The Japanese Government seemed to be aware of the significance of such coincidences and for at least twenty years it has bestowed gifts and courtesies on Peru. The Manco Kapac statue was one such gesture, perhaps a too transparent one. On the occasion of the fourth centenary of the foundation of Lima in 1935, Japanese residents presented the

[2] In other words, the Japanese colony is a well-organized group which could be utilized for political ends by an audacious and unscrupulous Japanese government. But it must be judged as an instrument, a means of policy, and not as possessed of a policy of its own, or, even less, an innate anti-Peruvian tendency. Peruvians are right in the main when they note the discipline and organization of the Japanese, their tendency to submit disputes to their consular authorities, and their reluctance to invest in Peru. But they go too far when they say that the colony constitutes "una agresiva minoría que se prepara a dirigir en un futuro no lejano el rumbo del país, en provecho de la patria lejana" (*La Prensa*, Oct. 11, 1937). Utterly fantastic are the similar fears that, after studying in Japan, young Japanese return to take academic degrees in Peru, and thus infiltrate in the Peruvian ruling class (*ibid.*, Oct. 20, 1937). More credible seem the sober indictments of Ulloa, who helped to design the anti-Japanese immigration laws. He says that young Japanese go to Japan "con la indudable ayuda del Estado Japonés"; that, on their return, they act under the supervision of "elementos de autoridad propia, que son en última instancia el Estado Japonés"; and that there are without doubt "spies" and possibly "saboteurs" (what we should now call "fifth-columnists") among them (*op. cit.*, pp. 347, 350, 362).

town with a 65,000-sole swimming-pool (the *Piscina de Natación Japonesa,* now *Piscina Municipal* in the Lima Stadium). And when Japanese astronomers came to Peru to observe a solar eclipse in the Andes, they left their telescope and other instruments to San Marcos University on their departure. Again, when an earthquake shook Lima on May 24, 1940, the Japanese Government sent construction materials to the victims.[3]

In spite of all this, Peruvian public opinion continues to be rather anti-Japanese. In addition to the political suspicion, which remains the main factor, other motives enter into this deep-rooted attitude. For one thing, the strongest desire of the country is to develop its natural wealth. For this, capital is needed more than labor. Yet the Japanese did not bring capital; they brought labor, and would like to bring more. Moreover, even in this melting-pot of widely different races which constitute Peru, the Japanese are the most difficult to assimilate. Intermarriage is exceptional. Neither indigenous customs nor the Spanish heritage attract them. Even republican institutions and democratic ideals, painstakingly fostered in these lands of

[3] *Revista de Hacienda,* No. 5, pp. 111. Behrendt's descriptions (*op. cit.,* p. 3) of "the intensity and extensiveness of Japanese commercial, cultural and political propaganda (all three usually go together)" are somewhat exaggerated. To be sure, a great quantity of magazines, leaflets and illustrated folders are distributed free of charge, but their propaganda value is slight. It is doubtful whether pictures of flowers and Buddhist temples increase the sales of toothpaste or dried fish. One of Behrendt's statements—"scholarships for study in Japanese universities are given and invitations for visits to Japan by Latin Americans are numerous"—may be true of other Latin American countries, but not in general of Peru. Only two or three very small fellowships were granted about 1937.

CONCLUSION 125

autocratic traditions, remain unreal to the loyal subjects of the Son of Heaven.

Absorption has always been a slow and painful process in Peru. The *mestizo* is a new human type, and a good one, but his evolution was not easy. The assimilation of Negroes and Chinese, not to mention the millions of pure Indios in the Sierras, or the half-savage Amazon tribes, is still far from accomplished. From this point of view, the Japanese colony constitutes simply an additional problem for Peru.

The isolation of the Japanese colony is accentuated by another peculiarity. The Japanese in Peru believe that they have done their duty to their adoptive country because they are law-abiding citizens, able workers, punctilious business men. Individually speaking, they are justified in this belief. Nobody can ask more from a fellow-man. But, collectively, they owe Peru something more—and this they do not seem to realize. They work and earn and save—and that is all. To be sure, they entertain high moral sentiments and religious and patriotic ideals. But to the bulk of the Peruvian people, they appear *en masse* as tradesmen and cultivators, shopkeepers and artisans. The Italians gave Peru a Raimondi; the Americans, a Meiggs; the Germans, a Middendorf; etc. Not a single Japanese name has endeared itself to Peruvian national feeling, not a Japanese is known but for his mercantile activities.[4]

[4] Some of them, at least, have begun to feel such inferiority. The often quoted Ikeyama expressed in his last contribution to *La Prensa* (October 29, 1937) the hope that the Japanese colony will be able in the future to collaborate also in the cultural and intellectual fields. Until now the Japanese School, about which there has been so much argument, does not represent a "cultural" danger nor a cultural "hope": it is rather below the average level of local schools.

Is it any wonder, then, that cultivated Peruvian opinion should resent Japanese immigration, if a society which has always prized spiritual values should be inclined to exhibit impatience towards such a utilitarian community? This too can be remedied. It has happened in other cases. In a better international atmosphere, with more mutual toleration, it is well within the realm of the possibilities to stimulate the intercourse, the collaboration, eventually the full absorption of the small nucleus with all its high and enduring values, in the greater Peruvian nation.

BIBLIOGRAPHY

PERUVIAN IMMIGRATION PROBLEMS

Arona, Juan de (Pedro Paz Soldan y Unánue), *La Inmigración en el Perú,* Lima, 1891.

Brayce y Cotes, Luis N., *Resumen histórico acerca del desarrollo de la inmigración en el Peru,* Lima, 1899.

De la Fuente, C. A., "Inmigración y actividades de los japoneses en el Perú," Boletin del Ministerio de Relaciones Exteriores, XXXIV, 1937, No. 129, pp. 178-86.

Del Rio, Mario E., *La inmigración y su desarrollo en el Perú,* Introduction by Dr. Luis Varela y Orbegoso (Clovis), Lima, 1909.

Guevara, Victor J., "El Problema de la Inmigración Japonesa," in *Las grandes cuestiones nacionales,* Cuzco, 1939.

Leon Garcia, Enrique, *Las Razas en Lima,* Lima, 1909.

Pesce, Luigi, *Indígenas e inmigrantes en el Perú,* Lima, 1906.

Sacchetti, Alfredo, *Inmigrantes para el Perú,* Turin, 1904.

Tudela y Varela, Francisco, "El Problema de la Población en el Perú," *Revista Universitaria,* III, 1908, pp. 201-21.

OTHER JAPANESE-PERUVIAN PROBLEMS

Donham, W. B., "El Japón avanza," *Boletín de la Cámara de Comercio de Lima,* VI, 1935, pp. 443-447.

Lembcke, J. Bailey, "El Comercio Exterior del Japón en 1934," *Boletín de la Cámara de Comercio de Lima,* VI, 1935, pp. 214-16.

"El Progreso Industrial y Comercial del Japón," *Boletín de la Cámara de Comercio de Lima,* VI, 1935, pp. 71-2.

Loayza, Francisco A., Manko Kapac (El fundador del Imperio de los incas fué japonés), Twenty-second International Congress of Americanists, held in Rome. Pára, 1926.

Ulloa, Alberto, *Posición Internacional del Perú,* Lima, 1941.

ARTICLES PUBLISHED IN "LA PRENSA" IN 1937

Akio, Banno, "El Mejoramiento de la Raza y Inmigración Asiática," Sept. 20; Oct. 4.

"Asociación Nacional pro Marina," Aug. 27.

Badani, J., Oct. 30.

Brenner, Acha, Oct. 31.

Davila, J. P., "La Infiltración Japonesa," Oct. 11.

Editorials, Aug. 22 and Sept. 2.

Figueroa San Miguel, Pedro, Oct. 20 and 21.

Garcia, D. M., Nov. 1.

Gomez, Manuel Enrique, Sept. 1.

Gonzales, M. Pedro, "La Ocupación Japonesa de los valles de Huaral y Chancay," Sept. 4.
Gonzales Tello, J. Y. M., Oct. 14.
Hauser, H., "La Inmigración en el Brasil y el Problema Japonés," Sept. 9, 10, and 11.
Ikeyama, K., "Un punto sobre cada i," Sept. 13 and 17; "Nuevos puntos sobre nuevas ies," Sept. 25; "Un punto sobre cada i," Sept. 29; "Un punto sobre cada i: Inmigración Japonesa e industrias agrícolas Peruanas," Sept. 30.
La Infiltración Japonesas: Un punto sobre cara i: "Acerca del comercio Peruano-Japonés," Oct. 12; "Posibilidades de incremento comercial," Oct. 13; "Nuevos aspectos del comercio Peruano-Japonés," Oct. 15; "Nuevos conceptos sobre los mismos errores," Oct. 24; "Desde el comercio minorista hasta las Empresas Colonizadoras de la Montaña," Oct. 29; "Rectificación," Oct. 30.
"J. D. L.," Sept. 22.
Moreyra y Paz Soldan, Carlos Enrique, August 29; "La Penetración Japonesa en el Perú," Sept. 26 and Oct. 3.
Muñante Gomez, Jorge, Sept. 1.
Nosiglia, P., Oct. 2.
Olivares, Salvador, "El Mejoramiento de la Raza y la Inmigración Asiatica," Sept. 16, 24 and Oct. 17.
Palacios Arauco, M., Oct. 16.
Ramirez y Gonzales, J. M., Sept 18 and Oct. 1.
Romero La Fuente, Manuel, Aug. 24,
"S.," Aug. 31,

Salinas Cossio, G., "La Infiltración Japonesa," I, "La Colonia Japonesa y la Produción Agrícola," Aug. 21; II, "El Japón y el Comercio," Sept. 6; III, "El Comercio entre el Perú y el Japón," Sept. 28; IV, "La Colonia Japonesa—El Pequeño Comercio y la Pequeña Industria," Oct. 19; other articles, Sept. 14 and Oct. 6.
"X. Y. Z.," Aug. 27.
Zegarra, Enrique, Oct. 26.

INDEX

A

Acara, 41
Acaka, 42
Agriculture, 9, 12, 14, 37-42, 48, 52, 66-67, 71, 89
"Agro-Industrial Institute," 42
Alliance, 39
Alta-Paulista, 36
Alpaca wool, 104-105
Alta-Sorrocabana, 36
Amazon, State of, 36, 40, 42, 46, 56-57
Amazon Development Company, 42
Antimony, 18, 107
Anti-Slavery Law of 1871 (Brazil), 20
Aracatuba, 36
Argentina, Japanese in, 11, 15; trade with Japan, 16
Asia, Japanese in, 11
Australia, 26; trade with Japan, 17

B

Bakeries, 99
Bananas, 38
Bank of Japan, 41
Bank of Taiwan, 44
Banks, 111 and footnote
Bahiano, Dr. Henrique, 42
Bastos, 36, 39, 51-53
Bazuars, 92-98, 108-109
Beef, 17
Belém, 41, 42, 49
Benavides, President, 114
Birthrate, 84 and footnote
Blacklisting, 121 footnote

Bolivia, Japanese in, 11, 48; trade with Japan, 18
Bopp, Raul, 55
Brazil Takahoka Kumiai, 30
Brazil, attitude toward Japanese, 35, 47-58; foreigners in, 34; immigration policy, 19-26; Japanese in, 6, 11-12, 14, 19, 26, 32-53, 56-57, 72, 90; trade with Japan, 15-18, 53
Brazil Imin Kumiai, 26
Brazil Takushoku Kumai, 39
British Dominions, immigration policy, 8
Buddhism, 31, 40
Buttons, 14

C

Cacao, 41
Callage, Fernando, 50
Calderon, Garcia, 72-73
Camara, Aristoteles de Lima, 51
Callao, 75-76, 85
Canada, Japanese in, 11, 34, 48
Cañete, 70, 72
Capital goods, 109
Capital Investments, 13, 29, 43-45, 50-51, 53, 94, 97, 124
Cananeia, 36
Castanhol, 41
Catholicism, Roman, 31
Central America, immigration policy, 7
Cerro de Pasco, 85
Centro de Estudos Economicos, 55
Chacra Cerro, 72
Chancay Valley, 87-89, 100

131

132 INDEX

Chile, Japanese in, 11, 48; trade with Japan, 15-16, 18
Chillon Valley, 87
China, Japanese in, 11; trade with Japan, 17
Chinese, 4, 7, 8, 32, 48; in Brazil, 19; in Peru, 66, 68, 70, 73, 88, 92, 125; intermarriage, 83
Civil Service, 12
Cobalt, 18
Cocaine, 106
Coffee, 17, 20, 25, 37, 50, 52, 90, 106; shops, 99
Colegio Niponico, 32
Colonization, 3, 13, 19, 22-23, 25, 26, 28-33, 35-53, 72, 75, 82-91, 97
Colombia, 8; Japanese in, 11, 26, 48
Companhia Nipponica de Plantacão do Brazil, S. A., 41
Commerce, see Trade
Conto, Dr. Miguel, 21
Co-operative Societies, 29-30, 37, 40, 90-91
Copper, 17, 18, 67, 106
Corn, 42
Cornelio Procopio, 36
Cosmetics, 14
Costa Rica, 8
Cotia, 36
Cotton, 14, 17, 18, 20, 38, 40, 41, 43, 44, 52, 86-96, 105-106, 108-110, 119
Cotton textiles, 14, 96-97, 108, 118-120
Covarrubias, Diáz, 7
Crystal quartz, 18
Cuba, 26; Japanese in, 48

D

Depression, World, 8, 76
Diamonds, industrial, 18
Domestic service, 12

E

Ecuador, 104 *footnote*
Electric appliances, 14; bulbs, 14; power, 38

Emigration, Japanese, 6, 20, 66; character of, 9; management, 10; propaganda, 28-29; *see also* Japanese
Exchange control, 17
Exclusion Act, *see* Immigration Law of 1924

F

Farming, *see* Agriculture
Fifth-Columnists, see Subversive activities
Fishing, 38, 58
Flour, 52
Fluorspar, 19
Foodstuffs, 107-108, 109
Fruit, 42
Fukuhara, Hachiro, 32, 41

G

Gasoline, 106
Gentlemen's Agreement, 4, 7
Germany, colonization of, 23; immigrants from, 34, 56, 57; relations with Japan, 18; trade competition with Japan, 17; trade with Japan, 105; trade with Peru, 120-121
Glassware, 107-108
Gold, 20, 105
Great Britain, relations with Japan; trade with Japan, 105, 120 *and footnote;* trade with Latin-America, 13, 14, 113
Guama, 41
Guano, 88
Guatemala, 8
Guilds, *see* Co-operative Societies

H

Hardware, 108-109
Hawaii, Japanese in, 11, 24, 37, 69
Henequen, 19
Hides, 17, 18
Hirota, Koki, 22
Huachipa, 72
Huallaga, 91

INDEX

Huancayo, 81
Huanuco, 75
Huaral, 87

I

Ilha Grande, 58
Iguapé, 37, 38
Immigration, 34; restrictions, 4, 7-8, 21-22, 113-116
Immigration Law of 1924, U. S., 4, 7-8, 34-35, 45
Imports, see Foreign trade
Incas, 61-62
Indians, 32, 93
Industries, 14, 46, 97, 100
Insurance, 110
Intermarriage, 83-84, 124
Investments, 97
Iron, scrap, 18
Italy, immigrants from, 34, 56, 92; immigration policy, 20-21, 68

J

Japan, discrimination against, 113-121; emigration policy, 10, 24, 27, 34-35, 52, 65-66, 72, 74-75; expansion policy, 7, 35, 78-79; military strategy, 4, 17-18; relations with Germany, 17-18; relations with U. S., 73; ship subsidies, 13, 30-31; trade, 4, 13-15, 17-19, 27, 65-66, 77, 90, 96-97, 102-112
Japanese agriculture, 9, 12, 14, 37-42, 48, 52, 66-67, 71, 89; banks, 111 and footnote; colonies, 3, 13, 19, 22-23, 25, 26, 28-33, 35-53, 72, 75, 82-91, 97; industries, 14, 46, 97-98; investments, 97; labor, 3-4, 7, 9-10, 20, 24-26, 31, 37, 48, 67, 69-70, 72, 89, 100, 124; occupations, 9, 11, 37-38, 48, 70, 74, 76, 88, 91-92, 97, 122.
Japanese land-ownership, 25, 36-41, 77, 85, 97; residents, characteristics of, 9, 97-98, 101, 122-126; non-assimilation, 52-53, 56; number of, 5-6, 11-12, 26, 40-41, 72-75, 78-79, 82-83, 87; savings, 98, 111, 122; schools, 32-33, 42, 53; shipping, 110 and footnote
Jeronimo, S., 36
Jobim, José, 55
Junin, 75, 85
Jute, 43

K

Kaigai Iju Kumiai, see Co-operative Societies
Kagai Iju Kumiai Kengokai, 30
Kaigai Kogyo Kabushiki Kaisha, 26, 28-29, 37, 38, 39, 43-44, 52, 74
Kaigai Kyokai, 29
Kapac, Manko, 63-64, 123
Kanegafuchi, 41, 43
Kokoku Shokumin Kaisha, 25

L

La Aroya, 85
La Libertad, 85
Labor, 124; contract, 3, 20, 24-26, 31, 37, 48, 69-70, 72, 89; skilled, 100; demand, 4, 7, 9-10, 19, 24, 46, 67
Lambayaque, 85
Land ownership, 25, 36-41, 77, 85, 97
Laredo, 72
Latin America, 5-9; trade with United States, 14, 17, 18; see also South America
Lead, 106-107
Lima, 64; Japanese in, 75, 85, 86, 87, 92, 97, 99
Linen, 108
Lins, 32, 36
Loayza, Francisco A., 63
Londrina, 36
Lumber, 38

M

Madre de Dios, 75
Maize, 90

INDEX

Manchuria, Japanese in, 11; trade with Japan, 17
Mandioca, 38
Manganese, 18
Manufactured goods, Czechoslovakian, 107; Japanese, 14, 97, 107-108
Manufacturing, 12
Marilia, 36
Matto Grasco, 36, 46, 56
Mercury, 18, 19
Metals, 18-19; see also Minerals
Mexico, immigration policy, 7; Japanese in, 6, 8, 11, 48-49, 90; ships to, 31; trade with Japan, 16, 19, 27
Mica, 18
Minas Geraes, 36, 56-57
Minerals, 18-19, 67, 106
Minumo, Ryu, 25
Molybdenum, 18, 107
Morioka Imin Kaisha, 26, 69
Munitions, 110 and footnote
Myetsuka, Tsukasa, 42, 43

N

Nambei Shokumin Kabushiki, 25
Nambei Takushoku Kaisha, see South American Developing Company
Nationalism, 8, 22, 23, 61, 77, 122
Naturalization, 32
Negroes, 125
Nippon Yusen Kaisha, 30-31
Nitrates, 17
Noreste, 36
North America, Japanese in, 5, 11
Novelty goods, 97
Novo, Estado, 23

O

Oil, see Petroleum
Okuma, Count, 26
Osaka Mainichi, 37
Osaka Shosen Kaisha, 30-31
Overseas Development Company, Ltd, see Kaigai Kogyo Kabushiki Kaisha

Overseas Emigration Societies Act of 1927, 29
Overseas Societies, see Kaigai Kyokai

P

Panama, Japanese in, 48; trade with Japan, 16
Pará, 36, 40, 41, 46
Paramonga, 72
Paraná, 36
Paraguay, 8; Japanese in, 11
Parantins, 42
Pepper, white, 43
Perené, 91
Perfumes, 97
Petroleum, 17, 106
Peru, anti-Japanese legislation, 113-121; attitude toward Japanese, 61-62, 66, 71-73, 76-81, 121 footnote, 122; Chinese in, 66, 68, 70, 73, 88, 92, 125; cotton in, 14, 119; immigration policy, 3, 5, 26, 66-73, 77, 113-116; Japanese in, 6, 11, 26, 47, 49, 61-112; ship to, 31; trade with Great Britain, 113; trade with Japan, 15-19, 74, 76, 102-112, 117-121; U. S. relations with, 121 footnote
Peruvian Corporation, 90 and footnote
Philippines, Japanese in, 11, 26, 56, 69
Poland, immigrants from, 34
Polyculture, 43, 47, 52
Porcelain, 14, 107
Portugal, immigrants from, 34
Potatoes, 40, 42
Propaganda, 54-55

Q

Quartz, crystal, 18
Quinine, 91

R

Raw materials, 10, 13, 14, 17, 44, 53, 58
Rayon textiles, 14, 108

INDEX

Registro, 39-40
Religion, 31
Rice, 37, 38, 41, 42, 43, 85
Rimac Valley, 87
Rio de Janerio, 36, 37, 41, 44, 55
Rio Grande do Sul, 18
Romero, Silvio, 23
Rubber, 18, 42, 43, 44, 67
    boom, 73

S

Salavery, Felipe Santiago, 5
Salt, 107 and footnote
San Nicolás, 72
Santos, 36, 58
São Paulo, State of, 14, 22, 49-50, 53; Japanese in, 25, 32, 36-40, 49-50, 56-58
Schools, Japanese, 32-33, 42, 53
Scrap iron, 18
Settlements, see Colonies
Sharecroppers, 86-87
Shintoism, 31
Shipping, 54, 110 and footnote
Shoda, Kazue, 26
Silk, 38; textiles, 14, 97, 107
Silver, 18, 67
Sino-Japanese War, 78
Skins, 17
Sociedade Colonisadora do Brazil, 52
South America, immigration policy, 5, 7-8; Japanese in, 5, 11; nationalism, 8; trade with Japan, 15-16
South American Developing Company, 40-41
South Sea Islands, 26
Sporting goods, 97
Steamship companies, 30-31
Suassuhy Grand, 39
Subversive activities, 53, 57-58, 79-80, 123 footnote
Sugar, 17, 18, 20, 37, 38, 68, 70, 85, 106

T

Trade, 10, 12, 48, 53-56, 92-101; foreign, 4, 10, 13-19, 27, 65-66, 77, 90, 96-97, 102-112; missions, 27; restrictions, 17, 117-121; treaties, 66-67, 77, 104, 108, 117, 120
Tres Barros, 39
Tungsten, 18, 106
Tupan, 51

U

Ugarte, Manuel, 72
Ulloa, A., 114, 122 footnote
Uruguay, Japanese in, 11; trade with Japan, 15-17
United States, exclusion of Japanese, 4, 7-8, 34, 45, 75; Japanese in, 11, 24, 32, 48; relations with Japan, 73; relations with Peru, 121 footnote; trade with Japan, 105; trade with Latin America, 14, 17, 18

V

Vanadium, 18, 107
Vargas, Getulio, 22, 23, 46, 57-58
Vegetables, 38, 42
Velloso, Dr. P. Leão, 55
Venezuela, Japanese in, 11, 15-16, 48
Villa Nova, 39

W

War materials, 18-19, 108, 110
Wheat, 17
Wool, 17, 18, 105, 108; Alpaca, 104-105
World War I, 25, 27
World War II, 17-18, 56-58, 106

Y

Yanacones, see Sharecroppers
Yen, 76, 108
Yokohama Specie Bank, 44